X4

5|97

HIAWATHA

HIAWATHA
Founder of the Iroquois Confederacy

Nancy Bonvillain

Senior Consulting Editor
W. David Baird
Howard A. White Professor of History
Pepperdine University

CHELSEA HOUSE PUBLISHERS

New York   Philadelphia

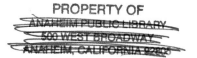

FRONTISPIECE   A depiction of Hiawatha wandering in grief. After the death of his three daughters, he left his Onondaga village and journeyed to Mohawk territory.

ON THE COVER   Hiawatha stands before a pole structure from which hang wampum strings. The bone comb on his chest is a reflection of one of the translations of the name Hiawatha: He Who Combs.

Chelsea House Publishers
EDITOR-IN-CHIEF   Remmel Nunn
MANAGING EDITOR   Karyn Gullen Browne
COPY CHIEF   Mark Rifkin
PICTURE EDITOR   Adrian G. Allen
ART DIRECTOR   Maria Epes
ASSISTANT ART DIRECTOR   Howard Brotman
MANUFACTURING DIRECTOR   Gerald Levine
SYSTEMS MANAGER   Lindsey Ottman
PRODUCTION MANAGER   Joseph Romano
PRODUCTION COORDINATOR   Marie Claire Cebrián

North American Indians of Achievement
SENIOR EDITOR   Liz Sonneborn

Staff for HIAWATHA
ASSISTANT EDITOR   Brian Sookram
COPY EDITOR   Ian Wilker
EDITORIAL ASSISTANT   Michele Berezansky
DESIGNER   Debora Smith
PICTURE RESEARCHER   Nisa Rauschenberg
COVER ILLUSTRATION   John Kahionhes Fadden

3   5   7   9   8   6   4

Library of Congress Cataloging-in-Publication Data

Bonvillain, Nancy
    Hiawatha: founder of the Iroquois confederacy/by Nancy Bonvillain
        p.   cm.—(North American Indians of achievement)
    Incudes index.
    Summary: Examines the life and career of the 15th century Iroquois Indian.
    ISBN 0-7910-1707-9
    ISBN 0-7910-1693-5
    1. Hiawatha, 15th cent.—Juvenile literature. 2. Iroquois Indians—Biography—
Juvenile literature. [1. Hiawatha, 15th cent. 2. Iroquois Indians—Biography.] I.
Title. II. Series
E99.I7H482 1992   91-20781
974.7'01'092—dc20   CIP
[B]   AC

CONTENTS

NORTH AMERICAN INDIANS OF ACHIEVEMENT

BLACK HAWK
Sac Rebel

JOSEPH BRANT
Mohawk Chief

COCHISE
Apache Chief

CRAZY HORSE
Sioux War Chief

CHIEF GALL
Sioux War Chief

GERONIMO
Apache Warrior

HIAWATHA
Founder of the Iroquois
Confederacy

CHIEF JOSEPH
Nez Perce Leader

PETER MACDONALD
Former Chairman of the Navajo
Nation

WILMA MANKILLER
Principal Chief of the Cherokees

OSCEOLO
Seminole Rebel

QUANAH PARKER
Comanche Chief

KING PHILIP
Wampanoag Rebel

POCAHONTAS AND CHIEF POWHATAN
Leaders of the Powhatan Tribes

PONTIAC
Ottawa Rebel

RED CLOUD
Sioux War Chief

WILL ROGERS
Cherokee Entertainer

SEQUOYAH
Inventor of the Cherokee Alphabet

SITTING BULL
Chief of the Sioux

TECUMSEH
Shawnee Rebel

JIM THORPE
Sac and Fox Athlete

SARAH WINNEMUCCA
Northern Paiute Writer and
Diplomat

Other titles in preparation

ON INDIAN LEADERSHIP

by W. David Baird
Howard A. White Professor of History
Pepperdine University

Authoritative utterance is in thy mouth, perception is in thy heart, and thy tongue is the shrine of justice," the ancient Egyptians said of their king. From him, the Egyptians expected authority, discretion, and just behavior. Homer's *Iliad* suggests that the Greeks demanded somewhat different qualities from their leaders: justice and judgment, wisdom and counsel, shrewdness and cunning, valor and action. It is not surprising that different people living at different times should seek different qualities from the individuals they looked to for guidance. By and large, a people's requirements for leadership are determined by two factors: their culture and the unique circumstances of the time and place in which they live.

Before the late 15th century, when non-Indians first journeyed to what is now North America, most Indian tribes were not ruled by a single person. Instead, there were village chiefs, clan headmen, peace chiefs, war chiefs, and a host of other types of leaders, each with his or her own specific duties. These influential people not only decided political matters but also helped shape their tribe's social, cultural, and religious life. Usually, Indian leaders held their positions because they had won the respect of their peers. Indeed, if a leader's followers at any time decided that he or she was out of step with the will of the people, they felt free to look to someone else for advice and direction.

Thus, the greatest achievers in traditional Indian communities were men and women of extraordinary talent. They were not only skilled at navigating the deadly waters of tribal politics and cultural customs but also able to, directly or indirectly, make a positive and significant difference in the daily life of their followers.

7

From the beginning of their interaction with Native Americans, non-Indians failed to understand these features of Indian leadership. Early European explorers and settlers merely assumed that Indians had the same relationship with their leaders as non-Indians had with their kings and queens. European monarchs generally inherited their positions and ruled large nations however they chose, often with little regard for the desires or needs of their subjects. As a result, the settlers of Jamestown saw Pocahontas as a "princess" and Pilgrims dubbed Wampanoag leader Metacom "King Philip," envisioning them in roles very different from those in which their own people placed them.

As more and more non-Indians flocked to North America, the nature of Indian leadership gradually began to change. Influential Indians no longer had to take on the often considerable burden of pleasing only their own people; they also had to develop a strategy of dealing with the non-Indian newcomers. In a rapidly changing world, new types of Indian role models with new ideas and talents continually emerged. Some were warriors; others were peacemakers. Some held political positions within their tribes; others were writers, artists, religious prophets, or athletes. Although the demands of Indian leadership altered from generation to generation, several factors that determined which Indian people became prominent in the centuries after first contact remained the same.

Certain personal characteristics distinguished these Indians of achievement. They were intelligent, imaginative, practical, daring, shrewd, uncompromising, ruthless, and logical. They were constant in friendships, unrelenting in hatreds, affectionate with their relatives, and respectful to their God or gods. Of course, no single Native American leader embodied all these qualities, nor these qualities only. But it was these characteristics that allowed them to succeed.

The special skills and talents that certain Indians possessed also brought them to positions of importance. The life of Hiawatha, the legendary founder of the powerful Iroquois Confederacy, displays the value that oratorical ability had for many Indians in power.

The biography of Cochise, the 19th-century Apache chief, illustrates that leadership often required keen diplomatic skills not only in transactions among tribespeople but also in hardheaded negotiations with non-Indians. For others, such as Mohawk Joseph Brant and Navajo Peter MacDonald, a non-Indian education proved advantageous in their dealings with other peoples.

Sudden changes in circumstance were another crucial factor in determining who became influential in Indian communities. King Philip in the 1670s and Geronimo in the 1880s both came to power when their people were searching for someone to lead them into battle against white frontiersmen who had forced upon them a long series of indignities. Seeing the rising discontent of Indians of many tribes in the 1810s, Tecumseh and his brother, the Shawnee prophet Tenskwatawa, proclaimed a message of cultural revitalization that appealed to thousands. Other Indian achievers recognized cooperation with non-Indians as the most advantageous path during their lifetime. Sarah Winnemucca in the late 19th century bridged the gap of understanding between her people and their non-Indian neighbors through the publication of her autobiography *Life Among the Piutes*. Olympian Jim Thorpe in the early 20th century championed the assimilationist policies of the U.S. government and, with his own successes, demonstrated the accomplishments Indians could make in the non-Indian world. And Wilma Mankiller, principal chief of the Cherokees, continues to fight successfully for the rights of her people through the courts and through negotiation with federal officials.

Leadership among Native Americans, just as among all other peoples, can be understood only in the context of culture and history. But the centuries that Indians have had to cope with invasions of foreigners in their homelands have brought unique hardships and obstacles to the Native American individuals who most influenced and inspired others. Despite these challenges, there has never been a lack of Indian men and women equal to these tasks. With such strong leaders, it is no wonder that Native Americans remain such a vital part of this nation's cultural landscape.

1

A VISION OF PEACE

Several hundreds of years ago, a man sat alone in a small clearing in the dense forests of what is now central New York State. He bowed his head and wept over the death of his three beloved daughters. Before him, he had erected two wooden poles and placed a third horizontally across them. The man had then hung three strings of small shells, some white and some purple, from the horizontal pole. Now, he sat near this structure, looked up at the strings of shell, and said:

> People boast what they would do in extremity but they do not do what they say. If I should see anyone in deep grief I would remove these shell strings from the pole and console them. The strings would become words and lift away the darkness with which they are covered. Moreover what I say I would surely do.

This is one report of a critical turning point in the life of Hiawatha (pronounced hi-ya-WA-ta), a chief of the Onondaga people. The Onondagas are one of five closely related Iroquois nations that inhabited the eastern woodlands long before European colonizers arrived in North America.

The Grief of Ainwatha (1983) shows Hiawatha holding a string of condolence beads as he mourns the death of his three daughters. This is one of many depictions of the Iroquois people by Mohawk artist John Kahionhes Fadden.

The events leading up to Hiawatha's journey through the forests and his later role in the formation of the Iroquois Confederacy are all recounted in the ancient narratives told by the Iroquois people. Because the Iroquois did not have a writing system, their histories were passed on orally from generation to generation. These accounts have been repeated by thousands of men and women during the past 500 to 600 years. As is only natural, the stories have sometimes been modified by their narrators. Some incidents were changed or omitted, and others were introduced or expanded. No one version of the life and deeds of Hiawatha is told by all Iroquois.

To people accustomed to learning about history from books filled with facts and dates, this may seem somewhat unsettling. But oral histories may be just as valid as written accounts. Even though some episodes may vary in the telling, major themes of traditional narratives are consistent. In addition, oral traditions of Indian peoples teach a valuable lesson: Precise facts about individuals are not necessarily crucial to an understanding of their life. What is possibly more important is gaining a sense of various individuals' role in the history of their people and knowing the contribution that their life has made to their society. Traditional stories told of Hiawatha and other important people in his era provide such a picture of the times in which he lived. These accounts also reveal the lasting meaning that his life and wisdom have had for all the Iroquois nations.

(Hiawatha's life has been greatly misconstrued as a result of the epic poem *The Song of Hiawatha* by Henry Wadsworth Longfellow. In 1855 the renowned poet wrote of the exploits of a legendary hero whom he mistakenly identified as Hiawatha. In actuality, Longfellow was recounting the adventures of a mythical figure of the Ojibwa people named Nanabozho.)

Hiawatha lived sometime between the late 14th and late 15th centuries. He made his home in one of the Onondaga villages, which were all located in central New York State in the middle of the vast territory inhabited

An illustration for The Song of Hiawatha, *Henry Wadsworth Longfellow's epic poem, which actually recounts the adventures of Nanabozho, a mythical Indian figure. This case of mistaken identity has led to much confusion about Hiawatha's life and achievements.*

by the five Iroquois nations. These groups settled in separate areas across the territory. To the east of the Onondagas were the Mohawks and the Oneidas. To the west were the Cayugas and the Senecas. They all spoke closely related languages belonging to the Iroquoian family. Because of frequent contact among the nations through trade, travel, and intermarriage, many people were bilingual or multilingual and were therefore able to communicate directly with members of other nations. In addition, Iroquois peoples shared many cultural practices, including methods of obtaining food, systems of family organization, rituals and religious beliefs, and ways of establishing unity and harmony in their villages.

Although the Iroquois nations had much in common, they also had disagreements and conflicts. At the time in which Hiawatha lived, these conflicts sometimes erupted into warfare. Feuds between families were the most common causes of hostilities. Such feuds seemed to have no end. They might start when someone killed another person, perhaps out of anger or jealousy. Then the victim's family would vow revenge against the murderer and that person's relatives. Either the murderer or someone from his or her family would be killed, leading to vows of vengeance by survivors.

When the original attack involved people from the same village, feuds were sometimes avoided by payment of gifts from the murderer's family to the victim's family as compensation for the crime. But attempts at reconciliation often failed. And if the people were from different villages or nations, feuds were the most frequent outcome. This strife often resulted in conflicts that continued for generations.

Although many of the Iroquois accepted this behavior as part of their way of life, Hiawatha was deeply troubled by hostilities that disrupted social harmony. He was saddened by such tragic loss of life. Hiawatha was a respected chief of the Onondagas and a great orator. He used his skills to speak to others about the senseless killings and dangers they brought to Iroquois survival. He thought too of the safety of his own three daughters whom he loved dearly, and he feared that someday they might be victims.

Hiawatha also knew that the Iroquois had outside enemies. Their lands were surrounded by the territories of other Indians with whom the Iroquois were occasionally at war. These people, most of whom belonged to Algonkian-speaking groups, such as the Mahicans, Algonquins, and Ottawas, had cultures that differed considerably from that of the Iroquois. Aware of the dangers to which they were exposed, the Iroquois built their villages on hilltops and erected defensive palisades around their settlements in order to protect themselves against intruders. From walkways along the tops of wooden palisades, they were able to see anyone approaching and could thereby prepare to repel an attack. Many Iroquois men went on armed campaigns against enemy warriors. They brought back captives if they were victorious and told the tales of their exploits. If Iroquois warriors were killed, their families would pledge renewed vengeance, continuing the deadly cycle.

Year after year, Hiawatha spoke eloquently of a different way of life, a way of peace and friendship. Many people listened to him and thought he was right, but still they were reluctant to change. Others, however, did not agree and opposed his every effort to establish harmony.

Violence among the Iroquois people and against neighboring enemies was a source of consternation for Hiawatha. He dedicated his life to achieving peace and unity for his people.

The person most antagonistic to Hiawatha's plans was a powerful Onondaga chief named Thadodaho (ta-do-DA-ho). He instilled fear in all who saw him, not only by the anger of his words but also by his strange appearance. It is said that he had snakes writhing in his hair and that his legs and arms were gnarled and crooked. Thadodaho's frightening appearance reflected the crooked paths of his mind, filled as it was with hatred and anger. His name, meaning "entangled," referred both to his body and his mind.

Thadodaho was known to have magical powers, which he used to injure or kill his enemies. He was supported by a group of warriors who gained prestige from their exploits and from their association with him. Although he was hated by many others, they were too afraid of him and his comrades to take any steps to counter his authority.

Hiawatha alone had no fear. He believed so strongly in the justice of his cause, the establishment of peace, that he refused to keep silent. His name itself signifies his mission. Some say the word *hiawatha* means "he who combs," referring to his desire to comb the snakes out of Thadodaho's hair, symbolically straightening his warped mind. Others say that it means "he who seeks something and knows where to find it," referring to his mission of peace.

Hiawatha decided to invite all in the village to come to a council to discuss his ideas. He wanted the villagers to publicly hear his words, and he wanted them to speak their mind on this matter. Many people attended the council because they too were distressed about conditions in their village. They had heard that Hiawatha had some plan to bring peace. Thadodaho also knew of the meeting and arrived just as people were beginning to speak in support of Hiawatha's plan. All fell silent. They knew that Thadodaho would seek revenge against anyone who dared to oppose him.

Soon afterward, one of Hiawatha's daughters became ill and died. No one knew the cause of her illness, but all suspected that Thadodaho's powerful magic had been the reason.

Hiawatha grieved for his daughter but was determined to continue to tell of his vision of a new society. He called together a second council. Some people who had attended the first meeting were afraid to come to another, but many others did arrive. So too did Thadodaho. His presence had the same effect as the first time. The meeting ended in silence.

Then, another of Hiawatha's daughters became ill and died, again for reasons unknown. Once more, Thadodaho's powerful magic was suspected as the cause.

Hiawatha grieved for his daughters, but still he tried to bring courage to his people's hearts. He called a third council, but this time no one came. The villagers had all heard of the fate of Hiawatha's daughters and feared the same end would befall them.

But still Thadodaho sought revenge against Hiawatha. One day while Hiawatha's third daughter was outside doing her chores, a strange and beautiful bird suddenly appeared over the village. Many village youths shot their arrows at the bird to bring it down. Finally, one young man succeeded, and the huge bird fell to the ground. As the crowd rushed to the place where the strange creature had fallen, they knocked down Hiawatha's daughter, who could not move quickly out of the way because she was heavy with child. Hiawatha's dearest daughter was trampled to death. Thus did Thadodaho satisfy his evil mind.

The traditional stories of the Iroquois express Hiawatha's reaction in these words (as quoted in the

constitution of the Iroquois Confederacy): "The grief of Hiawatha was terrible. He threw himself about as if tortured and yielding to the pain. No one came near him so awful was his sorrow. Nothing could console him and his mind was shadowed with the thoughts of his heavy sorrow."

"I shall cast myself away. I shall bury myself in the forest, I shall become a woodland wanderer," he said.

Hiawatha did as he had spoken. He left his village and wandered south and east toward the territory of the Mohawk people. He could think of nothing but the sorrow and anger he felt because of the death of his daughters.

Thadodaho was the most feared and powerful Iroquois chief in the time of Hiawatha. Thadodaho was said to have snakes writhing in his hair, as this 1980 soapstone sculpture of him by Cleveland Sandy, a Cayuga Indian, illustrates.

He was a man well past the prime of his life, and now he was all alone.

After several days' journey, he came upon a lake where he saw a flock of ducks numbering in the hundreds. He spoke to them, telling them to fly away. They obeyed his words, and as they flew up so suddenly and in such large numbers, they drew up the water of the lake into the air. As Hiawatha was crossing the dry lake bed, he noticed beautiful empty shells from freshwater snails. Some shells were white and others were purple. Hiawatha gathered up many of the shells and put them in a deerskin pouch that he carried with him.

In the evening, he came upon a clearing in the woods where a small hut had been erected for shelter, probably by hunters or travelers. Hiawatha made a fire for himself and took out the shells he had collected. He strung together three strands of shell beads and said:

> This would I do if I found anyone burdened with grief even as I am. I would console them for they would be covered with night and wrapped in darkness. This would I lift with words of condolence and these strands of shell beads would become words with which I would address them. Holding these in my hand, my words would be true.

Hiawatha had arrived at the end of one period of his life and at the beginning of another. The words that he spoke to himself in mourning have become the essence of the great rituals of condolence that the Iroquois have repeated countless times from those days until the present. The journey that Hiawatha undertook in his time of personal tragedy paved the way for the development of the Iroquois Confederacy, an institution dedicated to peaceful cooperation among the Iroquois nations. During the centuries that followed, the confederacy Hiawatha helped to found would have a dramatic and decisive impact on the course of North American history.

The Peacemaker saying good-bye to his mother and grandmother as he embarks, probably at the Bay of Quinte, to sail around Lake Ontario to Mohawk country.

2

ᐁ ᐁ ᐁ

MEETING OF THE FOUNDERS

Early one morning, after Hiawatha had found shelter near a Mohawk village, a young girl noticed smoke coming from a hut in the woods. When she told her father that she had seen an unknown man in the hut, he said: "The stranger must be Hiawatha. I have heard that he has departed from Onondaga. Return, my daughter, and invite him to our house."

When Hiawatha arrived in the village, the people were in the midst of a council meeting. Hiawatha was invited to attend. He did so, but after several days of discussion, no conclusions were reached. Disagreement arose over every issue with no attempts at compromise or unity. Hiawatha was dismayed and decided to continue his journey.

After several more days of wandering, he camped near another Mohawk village. Again he was discovered by inhabitants and welcomed as a guest. He attended councils in this village, but again the speakers were unable to resolve their disagreements. Once more, Hiawatha departed in sadness.

As Hiawatha camped in a third place, he was observed by a woman who was out fetching water from a nearby spring. When she returned to her lodge, she reported to her husband that she had seen a man sitting motionless in a clearing in the woods. One of the people present in the house was a man named Deganawida (de-ga-na-WEE-da). (This man has since been called the Peacemaker because of his role in helping to found the Iroquois Confederacy. He is now always referred to by that name whenever Iroquois people speak of him.) When he learned of Hiawatha's presence in the woods, he told a young man in the village: "It is a guest. Go and bring him in. We will make him welcome."

Some say the meeting between Hiawatha and the Peacemaker was foretold in a prophecy. A powerful seer had once said that these two wise men would one day meet and through their efforts a great peace would be established.

The Peacemaker, like Hiawatha, was a wanderer. He was born in the north and eventually found his way to Mohawk territory. It is said that the Peacemaker was a member of the Wendat nation (later called the Hurons by Europeans). The Wendats resided in fertile lands on the northern shores of Lake Ontario, east of Lake Huron. They were distantly related to the Iroquois people and spoke a language that was similar to those of the five Iroquois nations. The Wendat and Iroquois cultures also resembled each other in their reliance on farming and hunting for subsistence, their systems of family organization, and their religious beliefs.

One story tells of the Peacemaker's miraculous birth. It is said that his mother was a young woman who lived with her mother among the Wendats. The two women were the last members of their families. They lived by themselves, bereft of the large kinship groups that nurtured most Wendat people. The young woman was not married and had no friends. One day, her mother noticed that she looked pregnant. The daughter said that she was indeed with child but had no idea how it had happened because she had never been with any man. Her mother did not believe what she said and accused her of promiscuity. The daughter was distraught and spent many of her days in weeping.

In some versions of the story, a spirit messenger came to the young woman in a dream (and in other versions, to her mother) telling her that when the baby grew up he would leave his homeland and travel south to the Mohawks. It was said that the Peacemaker would bring about changes that would indirectly lead to the destruction of Wendat society.

When the baby was born, his grandmother sought to kill him so that he would not fulfill the prophecy. She took the baby, cut a hole in a frozen lake, and threw him into it to drown. However, the boy did not sink into the freezing water and was not harmed. Twice more the grandmother tried and failed to kill him. Both grandmother and mother became convinced that the boy had special powers, and the grandmother never again tried to harm him. His mother was especially devoted to the boy and nurtured him throughout his childhood. The child grew to be a handsome youth. But he suffered from a speech impediment, which caused him to stammer.

Like the Iroquois nations, the Wendats were often at war with other peoples. And like the Iroquois, conflicts and feuds continually erupted within villages. By the time the Peacemaker grew to adulthood, it was clear that he was very different from most Wendat men. The others were all caught up in cycles of warfare and retaliation, but the Peacemaker took no interest in such exploits. He tried to point out the futility of such behavior. He tried to show his people the way toward peace.

But other Wendats thought that the young man who spoke of peace was odd. They did not understand his message. Finally, the Peacemaker realized that he could

never convince his own people to abandon their desire for war. As the messenger had foretold, he bid farewell to his family, saying: "I shall now build my canoe, for the time has come for me to set out on my mission in the world. I go seeking the council smoke of nations beyond this lake, holding my course toward the sunrise. It is my business to stop the shedding of blood among human beings."

The young man told his mother and grandmother that he would never return but if they wanted to know about his safety, they should cut a gash into a certain tree and if blood flowed from the cut, they would know he had died without accomplishing his mission. If no blood flowed, they would know that he was alive and well. Then the Peacemaker left his homeland and journeyed around Lake Ontario to the south.

On his travels, he came upon the lodge of a woman named Jikonsahseh (ji-gon-SA-seh) who was a chief among the Neutral nation. The Neutrals were also an Iroquoian-speaking people who lived southwest of Lake Ontario. Jikonsahseh's house was situated along a frequently used trail. Many travelers and hunters knew that they could receive food and shelter there. Jikonsahseh extended her generous hospitality to the Peacemaker. He accepted and then told her of his mission to unite the nations in a confederacy of peace:

> The Great Law that I bring is that all peoples shall love one another and live together in peace. This message has three parts—Good Word, Health, and Power: Gaiwoh (GA-ee-wo), Skenon (SGE-non), and Gashasdensaa (ga-shas-DEN-sa-a). And each part has two branches.
> Good Word means truth, justice, and right behavior practiced between people and between nations; it also means a desire to see justice prevail.
> Health means soundness of mind and body; it also means peace, for that is what comes when minds are sane and bodies cared for.
> Power means authority, the authority of law and custom, backed by such physical strength as is necessary to make justice prevail; it means also religion and ritual, for justice enforced is the will of the Holder-of-Heavens.

Then Jikonsahseh replied: "Your message is good. I take hold of it. I embrace it."

She told the Peacemaker to go forth on his journey to put these great words into action. The Peacemaker told Jikonsahseh that she too could put the words into action by refusing to give food and shelter to warriors along the path. Jikonsahseh agreed and therefore also became a worker for peace.

Before departing on his journey, the Peacemaker gave Jikonsahseh the title of Mother of Nations, Great Peace Woman. He told her: "You shall be the custodian of the Good Words of Peace and Power so that the human race may live in peace."

Jikonsahseh thus played an important role in the founding of the confederacy. She was the first person to hear the Peacemaker's plan. Her name, meaning "new face," signifies the new ideas and new way of life that she accepted. In addition, her encouragement and approval of the Peacemaker's message symbolized the necessity of gaining women's consent to decisions and actions taken by the confederacy. Finally, Jikonsahseh's refusal to feed warriors found its parallel in actual Iroquois behavior. Whenever a woman opposed her son's or husband's intention to go to war, she withheld the supply of dried corn bread that women usually provided for their kin. This symbolic act helped deter men from pursuing war.

After traveling for some time, the Peacemaker arrived at last in Mohawk territory and took up residence there to begin his work of peace. Because they were the easternmost of the Iroquois peoples, the Mohawks had to constantly guard their villages against enemies such as the powerful Mahicans who lived southeast of Mohawk lands in the Hudson Valley region.

When the Peacemaker arrived among the Mohawks and began to tell of another way of life, a way of peace, the Mohawks were skeptical about his message. However, they were willing to listen and think about his words. The newcomer offered them a test of his powers. He said that he would climb to the top of a pine tree on a cliff

A rendering in pen and ink of Jikonsahseh, the Great Peace Woman, who lent much support to Hiawatha and the Peacemaker in founding the Iroquois Confederacy. Behind her stands the snake-haired Thadodaho.

overlooking the deep Mohawk River. He told Mohawk leaders to chop down the tree so that he would fall into the churning water below. If he were killed, they would know that his message was false, but if he survived, they should believe his words. The chiefs did as he suggested. After seeing the Peacemaker's body fall into the river, they went back to their village, assured that he was gone forever. By nightfall he had not returned, so the Mohawks were certain that he had been killed.

According to one account quoted in the constitution of the Iroquois Confederacy: "The next morning some villagers saw strange smoke arising from the smoke hole of an empty cabin. They approached cautiously and peering in the side of the wall where the bark was loosened they saw the Peacemaker. He was alive and was not a ghost and he was cooking his morning meal."

The chiefs then realized that the Peacemaker had special powers and special knowledge. One Mohawk leader exclaimed: "Yesterday I was in doubt. Now I am in doubt no longer. Let us accept the message. Let us take hold of the Good News of Peace and Power."

The Mohawks knew that when the Peacemaker talked of peace he spoke from his heart, not from personal interest. He took no sides, favored no faction. The Mohawks understood that his words were true. They accepted his message and hoped someday to see it embraced by all the Iroquois nations.

The Peacemaker was so kind and wise that the Mohawks happily adopted him as one of their own. Years later, when Hiawatha was welcomed by the Peacemaker, the two men both had their minds set on accomplishing the same mission. They began to work together toward establishing peace and unity.

Hiawatha told the Peacemaker of his own hopes for peace. He wanted to find a way to resolve the endless feuds that constantly erupted among the people. Hiawatha told of the belligerent Thadodaho and of his wicked magic that killed his beloved daughters. He said, "It was truly a great calamity and I am now very miserable. My sorrow and my rage have been bitter. I can only rove about since now I have cast myself always from my people. I am only a wanderer."

The Peacemaker replied with kindness, "Dwell here with me. I will tell the others of your sorrow."

While Hiawatha remained in the lodge, Mohawk villagers met in council to discuss his sadness and to seek a remedy. They promised to follow whatever plan the Peacemaker and Hiawatha devised to establish peace and harmony.

When the council ended, the Peacemaker approached the house where Hiawatha waited. He saw the sad man

The Peacemaker condoling Hiawatha with a string of shell beads. For hundreds of years, the Iroquois people have used this ritual to end the grief of those suffering from the loss of a loved one.

sitting before the poles from which he had hung three strands of white and purple shells. And he heard Hiawatha say: "It is useless, for the people only boast what they will do but they do nothing at all. If what has befallen me should happen to them I would take down the three shell strings from the upright pole and I would address them and I would console them because they would be covered by heavy darkness."

The Peacemaker walked up to Hiawatha and took the three strands of shells from the pole. He offered one string to Hiawatha and said:

> When a person has suffered a great loss caused by death and is grieving, the tears blind their eyes so that they cannot see. With these words, I wipe away the tears from your eyes so that now you may see clearly.

Then the Peacemaker offered a second string of shells, saying:

> When a person has suffered a great loss caused by death and is grieving, there is an obstruction in their ears and they cannot hear. With these words, I remove the obstruction from your ears so that you may once again have perfect hearing.

At last, the Peacemaker offered the third string of shells to Hiawatha and said:

> When a person has suffered a great loss caused by death, their throat is stopped and they cannot speak. With these words, I remove the obstruction from your throat so that you may speak and breathe freely.

Hiawatha's eyes became clear so that he could see. His ears became clear so that he could hear. And his throat became clear so that once again he could speak eloquently. His mind was straight and strong. His courage returned.

The ceremony of condolence that the Peacemaker first performed in response to Hiawatha's grief has been repeated on thousands of occasions, upon the death of Iroquois people. It symbolically unites bereaved family members and others within their community. Those most touched by grief cannot perform the ritual for themselves because their eyes, ears, and mind are too clouded by sadness to function properly. They depend upon "clear-minded" people in their community to help them cope with their sorrow.

Some Iroquois tell of the meeting between Hiawatha and the Peacemaker in a different way. This version gives the same accounts of Hiawatha's life among the Onondagas, his conflict with Thadodaho, and the death of his three daughters. But it differs in its description of the first encounter between the two men. According to this account, one day during Hiawatha's journey east toward Mohawk territory, the Peacemaker, who was out hunting in the forest, came upon Hiawatha's hut in a clearing. The Peacemaker climbed up onto the roof of the hut and peered in through the smoke hole to see who was inside. He saw Hiawatha cutting up a human body and putting it into a kettle to cook. As Hiawatha looked into the kettle, he saw a reflection of the Peacemaker's face. The Peacemaker was extremely handsome, and his face had a look of kindness and wisdom. Hiawatha, thinking that the face reflected in the kettle was his own, wondered how someone with such beauty and kindness could want to eat human flesh. He exclaimed: "This is a most wonderful thing. I did not know I was like that. It was a great man who looked at me out of the kettle. It is my own face in which I see wisdom and righteousness and strength. But it is not the face of a man who eats humans. I see that it is not like me to do that."

Then Hiawatha took the kettle outside and emptied the contents near the roots of an upturned tree. He said, "Now I have changed my habits." He resolved never

Hiawatha sees the reflection of the Peacemaker's handsome, kind face and, thinking it is his own, decides to give up cannibalism. This is one version of the meeting of the two founders.

again to be a cannibal. Just then, the Peacemaker descended from the roof. When the two men met, Hiawatha told the Peacemaker of his decision. The Peacemaker then went hunting in the forest and caught a deer and brought it back to Hiawatha. He said that deer meat should be the food of humans.

Later, Hiawatha told of the events at the Onondaga village that had led him to leave his homeland. At this point, the two versions of the meeting between Hiawatha and the Peacemaker resume their common path.

Although the stories differ in some details, the crucial point is that both Hiawatha and the Peacemaker desired to establish peace and justice among the Iroquois nations. The second account has the element of cannibalism, a practice that may have been followed by Iroquoian peoples many centuries ago. By the time of European colonization and the beginning of written historical records in North America, eating human flesh had become one of the rituals associated with warfare. When warrior captives from other nations were brought back to Iroquois villages, they were sometimes killed and parts of their bodies were eaten in the victory celebration. The Iroquois believed that the strength and courage of a warrior was located in his body and was transferred to the victor in the process of eating. These beliefs and practices may have lasted into the 17th century.

Hiawatha and the Peacemaker were both dedicated to the pursuit of peace among the Iroquois. But traditional accounts indicate that the Peacemaker had a more concrete plan to put his thoughts into deeds. In fact, when he first told Jikonsahseh, the Great Peace Woman, of the words of his Message of Peace, she said to him: "A word is nothing until it is given form and set to work in the world. What form shall the message take when it comes to dwell among people?"

In response, the Peacemaker set forth his plan:

> It will take the form of the Longhouse in which there are many fires, one for each family, yet all live as one household under one chief mother. Hereabouts are five nations, each with its own council fire, yet shall they live together as one household in peace. They shall be the Kanonsionni (ga-non-SHON-nee), the Longhouse. They shall have one mind and live under one law. Thinking shall replace killing, and there shall be one commonwealth.

In symbolic form, these words spell out the basic structure of the Iroquois Confederacy. They also make a connection between the new league and the traditional way of life of Iroquois peoples. Iroquois households were composed of extended families living together in large rectangular structures called longhouses. These houses were built of poles from cedar trees that were covered with sheets of bark from the elm tree. They measured approximately 100 feet in length and 25 feet in width; some were even larger. The interior of a longhouse was divided into areas separated by partitions for the privacy of each family. A central row of hearths was located down the length of the house. Each hearth was shared by two families, who dwelt on opposite sides. Houses typically contained five or six hearths. Therefore 10 or 12 families usually lived within each longhouse. Shelves were built along the inner walls of the house about a foot from the ground. They were used for sleeping at night and for sitting or resting during the day. A higher row of shelves served to store equipment and food.

The interior of a longhouse. It was the Peacemaker's goal that all Iroquois people would "live together as one household in peace," similar to the way extended families shared the longhouse.

The Peacemaker used the image of the longhouse as a symbol of relationships among the Iroquois nations. Just as families within a longhouse are related to each other through kinship, loyalty, and cooperation, so too are the Iroquois nations related historically through their descent from one ancient people. Just as families rely on each other for aid, the nations too should follow principles of mutual support, protection, and generosity.

The Peacemaker incorporated into the league's structure the Iroquois principle of relationships through women. In Iroquois culture, families are related on the basis of matrilineal descent (*matri* meaning "mother" and *lineal* meaning "line" or "descent"). Individual families are associated through a grouping called a "lineage," which is composed of descendants of an elder woman. Children are born into the lineage of their mother. In the days of Hiawatha and the Peacemaker, these grouped families, or lineages, formed one household and resided together in a longhouse under the direction of its senior woman. After marriage, women remained in the household of their birth, whereas men moved into their wife's home. Therefore, a household generally consisted of an elder woman, her husband, their daughters, daughters' families, and the senior couple's unmarried sons.

Beyond this domestic unit, lineages belong to larger kinship groups called clans. A clan is composed of people who consider themselves related, although they may not be able to trace actual descent. Clan members believe themselves to be descendants of a common ancestor in the ancient past. As in the case of lineages, clans are traced through women. A child belongs to his or her mother's clan. According to Iroquois custom, two people of the same clan cannot marry each other, so one's father can never belong to one's own clan.

Three generations of Iroquois women. According to Iroquois tradition, the family line is passed on through women. Thus, all children are born into the lineage of their mother.

Iroquois nations have as many as 10 clans, although some nations, such as the Mohawks and the Oneidas, have only 3. Most clans are named after animals and birds, such as the Bear Clan, Wolf Clan, Turtle Clan, and the Hawk Clan. Two clans have the names of objects: Calumet and Ball.

Clans owned the longhouses in which their members lived. They also owned the surrounding land. Iroquois economies were based on a division of labor by gender. Women were the farmers. In spring, they planted crops of corn, beans, squash, melons, and sunflowers. They weeded their plants throughout the summer and harvested crops in autumn. Women also gathered wild berries, potatoes, and roots growing in natural abundance throughout Iroquois territory. Men provided their families with the meat of animals, fish, and birds that they caught in forests and numerous rivers and lakes.

The Peacemaker's plan for the confederacy also incorporated traditional Iroquois practices of discussion and

negotiation through councils. Before the era of the
founders, councils were held in each village to discuss
local problems, to settle disputes, and to plan communal
events such as funerals and other rituals. The Peacemaker
recognized the value of these local councils and used them
as building blocks in the structure of the league. For this
reason, when he described the league to Jikonsahseh, the
Peacemaker spoke of unifying the council fires of the five
Iroquois nations into one common group.

After Hiawatha and the Peacemaker met, their lives
and deeds became intertwined. Many tales recount
episodes that sometimes highlight the doings of one hero
and sometimes those of the other. Whereas some versions
place Hiawatha in prominence, others stress the role of
the Peacemaker. But in all the traditional accounts, the
aspirations and goals of the two men are united on the
same mission.

Stories about Hiawatha and the Peacemaker are symbolically related to the complex epics of creation told by
the Iroquois peoples. These myths tell of an ancient time
when there was no earth but only sky and water. In the
sky dwelt a woman with her husband. One day, she was
out gathering food near an enormous tree that had huge
roots spreading out in all directions. As she dug around
the roots, a large hole opened up in the sky and the
woman fell through it, descending toward the water
below. The woman feared that she would die. However,
birds in the air and creatures of the sea saw her falling
and decided to save her life. A muskrat quickly dived to
the ocean floor and pulled up some mud to place on the
back of a large turtle. The muskrat died in the attempt,
but other animals retrieved the mud from the muskrat's
paw and put it on the turtle's back. This mud provided
a soft place for the woman to land. The mud expanded
and eventually formed the earth.

Soon afterward, the woman gave birth to a daughter. When the daughter grew up, she too became pregnant and gave birth to twin sons. One son, the "right-handed" boy, was born in the normal manner, but the "left-handed" boy was born through his mother's armpit, killing her in the process. When the twins' grandmother saw what happened, she buried her daughter. And from the woman's body grew the plants of corn, beans, and squash, which have henceforth sustained the Iroquois peoples. These crops have since been called Our Life Supporters or the Three Sisters.

The twins proceeded to create various animals and plants. But they did not work in harmony. They hated each other and competed in all their endeavors. The right-handed twin was called Sapling because he was straight, soft, and flexible as a young tree. He created good things such as berries and fruits. The left-handed twin was called Flint because he was brittle and stubborn. He made briars and poison ivy. Sapling made rivers and streams flow in two directions so that humans could easily journey to wherever they wanted. But Flint changed the course of water so that rivers flowed only in one direction, making it difficult for people to travel.

The twins continually fought each other. After many battles, just as Sapling was about to kill his brother, he changed his mind and spared Flint's life. The two brothers represent the good and evil that exists in the world.

There are parallels between stories of Hiawatha and the Peacemaker and the creation myths. Like the twins, the Peacemaker was born to a woman who lived alone with her mother. Men do not figure prominently in the beginnings of either story. Like the twins, the Peacemaker was destined to wander throughout the world on a mission of creation. But whereas the twins created animals, plants, and material objects, the Peacemaker's goal was to create

a lasting social and political institution that would serve the Iroquois people.

Hiawatha and the Peacemaker are like the twins in their importance in shaping the world in which people live. But unlike the twins, who were always at odds, the two men were both dedicated to the common goal of achieving peace and harmony.

The relationship between Hiawatha and Thadodaho, the powerful Onondaga chief, is similar to that of the right-handed and left-handed twins. The two men had the same birthplace because both were Onondagas. Indeed, some versions of Hiawatha's life tell that he and Thadodaho were half brothers. In any case, like the twins, they each had a different vision of the type of world in which they wanted to live. Whereas Hiawatha yearned to establish harmony and unity, Thadodaho only wished for conflict. Like the twins, the two men competed with each other. Thadodaho tried to undermine all the good that Hiawatha wanted to create. Just as Flint tried to counteract the positive creations of Sapling, Thadodaho appeared at the Onondaga council meetings to destroy Hiawatha's plans for peace.

Whereas the Iroquois often speak of Sapling as the twin with the straight mind, they say Flint had a crooked mind. Like Flint, Thadodaho's mind was crooked, just as his body was gnarled and bent. Like Sapling, Hiawatha's mind was clear and straight.

Through these various stories, the Iroquois express their views of the world and their sense of what motivates people in their thoughts and actions. It is a world of turbulence and tension but one where the hope of balance and unity prevails. The Iroquois believe that people with clear and straight minds, like Hiawatha and the Peacemaker, will always act to bring about peace and harmony.

Fadden's acrylic painting Creations Battle *(1980) shows the struggle between the twins Flint and Sapling at the time of the creation of life on earth.*

3

NEGOTIATING THE UNION

After the Peacemaker condoled Hiawatha in the Mohawk village, he said, "My younger brother, your mind being cleared and you being competent to judge, we now shall make our laws and when all are made we shall call the organization we have formed the Great Peace. It shall be the power to abolish war and robbery and bring peace and quietness."

Hiawatha realized that he had finally found someone who was as committed to establishing peace among the Iroquois nations as he was. And so he replied, "What you have said is good. I do agree."

Then the Peacemaker said, "My younger brother, since you have agreed, I now propose that we compose our Peace Song. We shall use it on our journey to pacify Thadodaho. When he hears it his mind shall be made straight. His mind shall then be like that of other people."

Again Hiawatha responded, "I do agree, I truly believe the truth of what you say."

Then they sang their Song of Peace: "Hail! Hail! To the Great Peace, we bring greeting!"

Hiawatha and the Peacemaker discussed what they should do next in order to make real their vision of peace and unity. They decided to present their plan to the Mohawk council. The Peacemaker said, "We shall tell

The Council with Thadodaho When the League Was Started, *a 1936 tempera by Seneca artist Ernest Smith. Here, Hiawatha and the Peacemaker try to convince Thadodaho to accept their message of peace.*

our plan for a confederation and the building of a house of peace."

The two men returned to the Mohawk council and spoke about the Great Peace. Because the Peacemaker stammered, he relied on Hiawatha's skills as an orator to argue eloquently for the adoption of their peace plan.

Hiawatha told of the Great Peace and the Longhouse, wherein the Five Nations would live in peace and unity. The Mohawk councillors listened and all welcomed the proposal. In gratitude for Hiawatha's efforts to bring about lasting peace, the Mohawk council decided to adopt him as a member of their own nation. Then they asked Hiawatha and the Peacemaker to go forward and secure agreement from councils of the other four nations.

The first people to be approached were the Oneidas, whose lands were nearby, to the west of Mohawk territory. When their principal chief, Odatshedeh (o-DAT-se-de), whose name means the "quiver bearer," was told of the Great Peace, he replied, "I will consider this plan and answer you tomorrow." In symbolic Iroquois speech, "tomorrow" means "in a year."

The following year, Odatshedeh reported that the Oneida council had deliberated and found the Great Peace to be a good message. They decided to take hold of it and follow the words of Hiawatha and the Peacemaker.

Next, the leaders sent messengers to the Onondagas, who dwelt farther away, to the west of Oneida territory. Hiawatha knew that Thadodaho would refuse to join the Great Peace, but messengers were sent there nevertheless to try to convince him. As Hiawatha foretold, Thadodaho only looked at the messengers with scorn, refusing to even consider the proposal.

But the wise leaders of the Great Peace would not abandon their project. They decided to proceed westward

A representation of the Six Nations of the Iroquois Confederacy. From left: Seneca, Tuscarora, Cayuga, Onondaga, Oneida, Mohawk. The feather arrangement on each headdress is indicative of the respective nation.

and offer their plan to the Cayugas, who lived beyond the Onondagas. The Cayuga chief, Akahenyonk (a-ga-HEN-yonk), whose name means "wary spy," said that he would send word of response "tomorrow upon the midsummer day." At midsummer of the following year, the Cayugas too decided to join the Great Peace, saying, "We do agree with the Peacemaker and Hiawatha."

Next, Hiawatha proposed that all the chiefs from the Mohawk, Oneida, and Cayuga nations return to Onondaga and try again to win over Thadodaho. The Great Peace Woman, Jikonsahseh, also joined the group of ambassadors. It was decided that Hiawatha should use his eloquence and gifts of oratory to straighten Thadodaho's mind. The Peacemaker told Hiawatha, "I shall sing the Peace Song and you shall explain the Words of the Law, holding the wampum in your hand."

The group proceeded toward the Onondaga village. When they arrived in Onondaga territory, they halted their journey. In accordance with Iroquois custom, the travelers built a fire in a clearing so that the smoke would be seen and announce their arrival. Thadodaho sent messengers to greet them and discover their intentions.

The group of visiting chiefs representing the Mohawks, the Oneidas, and the Cayugas were joined by prominent Onondaga leaders who supported the Great Peace. This throng of people then approached Thadodaho's lodge. A man from among their group was chosen to sing the Hymn of Peace within earshot of Thadodaho. But the singer became so terrified of Thadodaho's power that he hesitated and faltered in his verses. The Peacemaker took his place and sang the hymn before Thadodaho's door.

When they were invited to enter, Hiawatha spoke to Thadodaho:

> Now look up and see the delegates of the Nations sitting around you, also see the chief warrior and this great woman, our mother Jikonsahseh, standing before you, all of whom have approved of this message. The chiefs and warriors and this great woman, our mother, have all agreed to submit the Good Words of Peace and Power to you.

Hiawatha continued:

> These are the Words of the Great Law. On these Words we shall build the House of Peace, the Longhouse with five fires that is yet one household. These are the Words of Righteousness, Health, and Power.

Hiawatha then offered concessions to Thadodaho's pride and vanity. He said that if Thadodaho joined the confederacy, the Onondaga village would be the meeting place for all future councils. The Onondagas would be known as the Fire-keepers and would have the honor of sending ambassadors to call the other nations to council meetings. Hiawatha promised Thadodaho that he would be considered the "first among equals." He would also have the privilege of announcing the opening of councils and declaring final decisions of the confederacy chiefs.

As Thadodaho listened to Hiawatha's words, all in attendance noticed that the writhing snakes in Thadodaho's hair ceased to move. His crooked limbs became straight and smooth. At last, he spoke: "It is well. I will now answer the mission which brought you here.

A meeting of confederacy chiefs. An important aspect of the league is that no decision is taken without unanimous approval or consensus of the chiefs.

I now truly confirm and accept your message, the object of which brought you here."

Thadodaho's response brought satisfaction to Hiawatha, the Peacemaker, Jikonsahseh, and the assembled chiefs of the four nations. The Peacemaker expressed the relief of all when he said, "We have now overcome a great obstacle. It has long stood in the way of peace. The mind of Thadodaho is now made right and his crooked parts are made straight."

Only one nation had yet to be approached for their consent to the Great Peace. Thadodaho suggested that they proceed to the land of the Senecas, the westernmost Iroquois nation. The Senecas comprised the most populous nation and were also extremely warlike. Because they had many enemies whose territories were located west among the Great Lakes, they always had to be on alert against attacks. The Senecas were led in war by two prominent chiefs—Kanyadariyo (ga-nya-da-RI-yo), meaning "beautiful lake," and Shadekaronyes (sa-de-ga-RON-yes), meaning "skies equal in length." Although many Seneca chiefs welcomed the founders' proposals for peace, these two leaders were opposed to the plan.

Hiawatha and the Peacemaker decided that it would be wise to offer concessions to these two Seneca chiefs in order to obtain their approval. Hiawatha told them:

> The chiefs of all Nations, together with their warriors, have unanimously accepted the message of Peace and Power and only you two chiefs have not yet accepted. The chiefs have unanimously decided to leave all the war power and military control of the people in your hands providing you accept the message so that in case of war with other nations you shall be the leaders of the people of the Confederate Nations in defense of their confederacy.

After listening to this proposal, the Seneca chiefs replied, "We are agreed to accept this message."

An Iroquoian longhouse. Several families lived together in these structures, which were about 100 feet long and 25 feet wide.

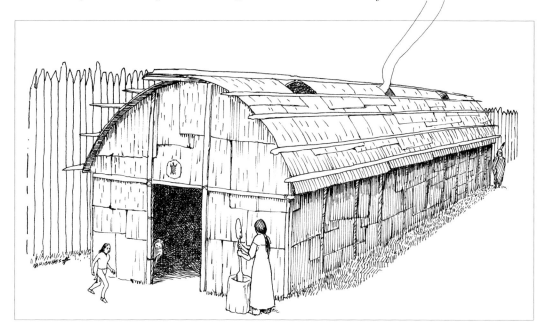

The Seneca chiefs accepted the responsibility of planning and organizing military operations. They took hold of the Great Message of Peace and Power. They pledged to follow it in harmony with the Five Nations.

Once agreement had been reached among the founders of the confederacy, Hiawatha and the Peacemaker asked each nation to appoint chiefs who would meet together and draw up the laws that would spell out the ways for the league to function.

Hiawatha gave each of the Five Nations a new name, symbolizing their new identity and rebirth into a different kind of society. In confederacy meetings, the nations are referred to by these names. The council name of the Mohawks is Tehadirihoken (de-ha-di-ri-HO-gen). This name means "two statements or ideas together" or "between two words." It is derived from the name of the leading Mohawk chief, Tekarihoken (de-ga-ri-HO-gen).

The Oneidas are called Nihatirontakowa (ni-ha-di-ron-da-GO-wa), or "those of the great log." The origin of this name comes from an episode during Hiawatha's journey to tell the Oneida chiefs of the Great Peace. Along the path, he had to cross a creek over which a large tree had fallen.

Hiawatha gave the Onondagas the name Rotisennakehta (ro-di-sen-na-GEH-da), which means "nominators," or literally, "they carry names on their shoulders." It originates from the fact that when new chiefs were brought into the league, the Onondaga leader Thadodaho called out the names of the candidates.

Next, Hiawatha named the Cayugas Sotinonnawentona (so-di-non-na-wen-DO-na), or the "great-pipe people," because one of the Cayuga chiefs brought a large peace pipe to the first council meeting.

Finally, Hiawatha gave the Senecas the name Ronaninhohonti (ro-na-nin-ho-HON-di), meaning "they who are at the doorway." This appellation derives from the Senecas' position as the westernmost nation and their role as the guardian of the door to the confederacy Longhouse from enemies to the west.

After negotiations were completed and all the nations had taken hold of the Great Words of confederation, Hiawatha saw that his vision was coming true. The Longhouse of the Great Peace was to be constructed. This Longhouse has one door facing the rising sun in the east. It is kept secure by Mohawks, who are thus known as Keepers of the Eastern Door. The Longhouse has another door facing the setting sun in the west, guarded by Senecas, the Keepers of the Western Door. And from the center smoke hole rises the warmth of the council fire at the Onondaga village, symbolizing the unity of the league.

Councils among Iroquois nations traditionally func-tioned on the basis of unanimity and consensus. These

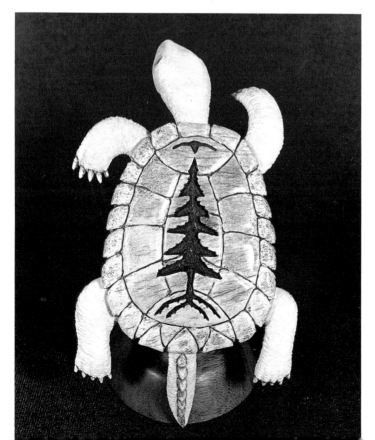

The Great Tree of Peace on the back of a turtle. The Peacemaker envisioned that all nations, spread out like the roots of a tree, would at the same time be joined together to forge one living structure.

two principles were incorporated into the confederacy as well. In village councils, whenever an issue was discussed, people were free to voice their opinions and explain their reasoning. No decisions were taken without unanimous approval. When disagreements arose, each person typically offered arguments in favor of his or her position. They hoped to convince those who were in the minority. Usually, given time and reasons, people eventually either came to agree with the consensus or were at least willing to publicly respect the majority position so that group action could be taken.

Hiawatha's skillful negotiations brought about the formation of the Iroquois Confederacy. Through his willingness to compromise and offer concessions to leaders like Thadodaho and the Seneca chiefs, Hiawatha was able to achieve his ultimate purpose. Most of these concessions were ceremonial in nature. No members of the league had more actual power than any others. However, Thadodaho was offered a publicly recognized and prominent ceremonial role when he was made the spokesperson for league announcements and decisions.

Hiawatha and the Peacemaker also enlisted the pressure of public opinion to win over Thadodaho. They convinced him that he alone stood in the way of a goal that the overwhelming majority of other Iroquois leaders desired. By confronting Thadodaho with the combined support of chiefs from the Mohawk, Oneida, and Cayuga nations, as well as that of many Onondaga leaders, Hiawatha and the Peacemaker severely limited Thadodaho's ability to go against public consensus.

Hiawatha's success in reforming Thadodaho is reminiscent of the relationship between the twins Sapling and Flint in the Iroquois creation story. Although the twins were in conflict during most of their life, Sapling was finally able to subdue Flint. Just as Sapling pacified Flint, Hiawatha was able to reform Thadodaho, who pledged

An eagle carved of moose antler by Stanley Hill, a Mohawk, in 1980. This bird is an important symbol for the Iroquois: It sits atop the Great Tree, looking out for the approach of enemies of the confederacy.

to use his skills to take a prominent role in the functioning of confederacy councils.

The league was born out of internal conflicts among the Iroquois nations. Its purpose was to put these conflicts to rest forever. The Peacemaker likened the league to a Great Tree of Peace, with four enormous white roots that spread out in cardinal directions to the east, south, west, and north. The roots spread throughout the world, uniting independent nations, which come together to forge one living structure.

In their first united act, members of the league buried their weapons of war under the White Roots of Peace. The Peacemaker thus spoke:

> We now uproot the tallest pine tree and into the cavity
> thereby made we cast all weapons of war. Into the depths
> of the earth, down into the deep underearth currents of
> water flowing into unknown regions, we cast all weapons of
> strife. We bury them from sight forever and plant again
> the tree. Thus shall all Great Peace be established and hos-
> tilities shall no longer be known between the Five Nations
> but only peace to a united people.

The White Roots of the Great Tree were lifted and weapons were thrown into the swift, cleansing stream flowing beneath the earth. Never again would confederacy nations take up arms against each other. And if any other nation struck a blow against a member of the league, the Iroquois believe that blood shall flow from the tree and all will be lost.

After the Five Nations had agreed to join the confederacy, the Peacemaker addressed them:

> I am the Peacemaker and with the Five Nations' Con-
> federate chiefs, I plant the Tree of the Great Peace. I plant
> it in your territory, Thadodaho, and the Onondaga Nation,
> in the territory of you who are Firekeepers.

> I name the tree the Tree of the Great Long Leaves. Under
> the shade of this Tree of the Great Peace we spread the
> soft white feathery down of the globe thistle as seats for
> you, Thadodaho, and your cousin chiefs.

This Great Tree and the nations that it nurtures and protects is guarded by an eagle who sits atop the tree and sees far and wide. If the eagle spots an enemy approaching the nations, it can warn the people to defend themselves.

The Peacemaker's image of the Great Tree has its parallel in the tree of the sky world whose roots opened up a hole in the heavens. It was through that opening that the woman of creation fell. Just as the tree of the sky world gave entry to beginnings of life on earth, the Great Tree of Peace symbolized a new beginning for the Iroquois nations.

4

THE GREAT BINDING LAW

Hiawatha and the Peacemaker came together with the assembled chiefs of the Five Nations to set forth the laws that would henceforth guide their relations. This body of rules is called Ne Gayanesha'gowa (ne ga-ya-ne-sa-GO-wa), or the Great Binding Law.

The Great Binding Law establishes procedures for the functioning of council meetings. If a member of any of the Iroquois nations wishes to have a matter discussed by the confederacy council, he or she informs one of the nation's chiefs. Then a messenger is sent to Thadodaho requesting that he convene the council. If Thadodaho deems the issue worthy of discussion, he sends messengers to announce the date for a meeting.

When all confederacy chiefs have assembled, they enter the council longhouse to deliberate. Inside, they arrange themselves in three areas. On one side sit the Mohawk and Seneca chiefs. On the other side sit chiefs representing the Oneidas and Cayugas. And in the center, before the council fire, are the Onondaga Fire-keepers.

In this illustration, a war club lies buried beneath the Great Tree, symbolizing the pledge of peace. As the Peacemaker spoke: "Into the depths of the earth . . . we cast all weapons of strife."

This seating arrangement symbolically mirrors the system of kinship organization that exists among Iroquois peoples. Iroquois clans are grouped into two moieties. A moiety (from the French word meaning "half") is an association of clans that divides a community or nation

53

into two groups. The 10 Iroquois clans are thus divided into 2 moieties. Moiety arrangements vary in each of the nations because not all clans are represented in every group. Generally, though, clans named after birds (Hawk, Heron, and Snipe) and the Deer clan form one moiety while clans named after other mammals (Bear, Beaver, and Wolf) and the Turtle clan comprise the other moiety. In similar fashion, the Five Nations of the confederacy are grouped into two sections. The Mohawks, the Onondagas, and the Senecas form one moiety, known as the Elders. The Oneidas and the Cayugas make up the Youngers.

The division of nations into moieties affects the order of deliberations at league meetings. When the confederacy council is convened, Thadodaho formally announces the opening of the meeting and declares the topic for discussion. Mohawk chiefs are first to deliberate among themselves. When they reach a united opinion, they pass the issue to the Seneca chiefs. These men then discuss the matter and announce their decision to the Mohawks. The Mohawks pass the matter "across the fire" to the Youngers moiety. The Oneidas deliberate next, followed by discussion among the Cayugas. Then their moiety's decision is passed to the Onondagas. If the two sides are in accord and the Onondaga chiefs agree, Onondaga Fire-keepers announce a unanimous decision. The chiefs have thus "rolled their words into one bundle."

However, if the Elders and Youngers differ in their opinions, the Onondagas either recommend a compromise or pass the matter again to the Mohawks for a further round of deliberations. If the Onondagas disagree with a joint decision of the Elders and Youngers, they may request that the matter be reconsidered. If additional deliberation results in the same opinion, the Onondagas accept the decision in the interest of consensus. Finally, though, if disagreement is widespread among the member nations, the matter is put aside and no action is taken. Lack of unanimity is symbolized by covering up the council fire, extinguishing the warmth of unity.

The system of negotiation at league meetings was based on principles of unanimity and consensus. It arose directly from Iroquois practices that had functioned previously in village councils throughout the nations. According to Iroquois ethics, no individual has the right

Chief addressing a council. When issues are discussed and a decision is reached, the chiefs are said to have "rolled their words into one bundle."

to compel others to act against their own wishes. Speakers attempt to justify their opinions in the hope of convincing others, but direct force or compulsion is considered contrary to the aims of unity and harmony.

When the chiefs who had been at the founding meeting heard the plan offered by Hiawatha and the Peacemaker, they decided that it was good. They all accepted the Great Binding Law and pledged to put it into action. Then the Peacemaker addressed the leading chiefs of each nation who had taken part in founding the confederacy. He asked them to appoint other members of their clans to join as councillors in the league.

He spoke to Hiawatha first: "You Hiawatha shall be first to come and appoint your colleagues; you are of the Turtle clan and shall therefore appoint your colleagues of the same clan."

Hiawatha chose two clansmen from among the Mohawk Turtle clan and answered: "This is now all ready, they have accepted."

Then, in succession, chiefs of the other Mohawk clans, the Oneidas, the Senecas, and the Cayugas selected their associates. Finally, Thadodaho appointed Onondaga chiefs to join the confederacy council.

Because of differences in the number of clans that existed in each of the Five Nations, the number of confederacy chiefs sent by each nation varies. There are 9 chiefs from both the Mohawk and Oneida nations; the Onondagas have 14; the Cayugas 10; and the Senecas 8. However, because chiefs from each nation deliberate among themselves and offer one united opinion, differences in the numbers of councillors representing each nation do not have an effect on the league's functioning.

When all was completed, the Peacemaker ceremonially installed each chief into the council by placing a head-dress of deer antlers upon the chief's head. Thadodaho

Iroquois chief wearing a deer antler headdress, a symbol of office within the league. Although chieftainships are held only by men, they are inherited and passed on by women—another aspect of the matrilineal tradition.

was the first to receive the symbols of office, followed in turn by the other 49 chiefs who took positions as officials of the confederacy.

At last, the Peacemaker spoke again: "We have now come to appointing the chiefs of the Five Nations. These chiefs have now all been crowned with deer's horns. Therefore we have now accomplished and completed the work of laying the foundation of the confederation."

The personal names of the 50 original confederacy chiefs have been retained as titles, which are assumed by their successors. When a chief dies, his title, or name, is inherited by another man within his clan. The plan for succession envisioned by Hiawatha and the Peacemaker relies on principles of clan inheritance that prevail among Iroquois peoples. Although chieftainships are held by men, they are inherited through women because Iroquois clans follow matrilineal descent.

The Great Binding Law spells out methods of succession. The Peacemaker said: "I now transfer and set over to the women who have the chief's title vested in them, that they shall in the future have the power to appoint the successors to fill vacancies caused by death or removals from whatever cause." In other words, when a chieftainship becomes vacant, senior women in the former chief's clan have the right to discuss together and decide on a successor to be appointed. These senior women are called "nobles," as are the chiefs. They have the duty of naming their candidate, who is then introduced to the council of the confederacy.

The duties of women within the league are extensions of their traditional roles in clans and households. The privilege of women to name confederacy chiefs derives from their control over inheritance in their families. The confederacy, then, makes use of Iroquois kinship relations. Principles of descent and leadership are transferred from households and local communities to a wider social and political context.

The genius of Hiawatha and the Peacemaker was that they did not try to impose an alien system on the Iroquois peoples. A foreign system would have been rejected or would have functioned in a limited way during a pressing emergency, only to be abandoned when specific dangers disappeared. Instead, the founders used traditional Iroquois practices to develop the confederacy, which was then supported and nurtured from within Iroquois culture.

In addition to the councillors, another set of chiefs was created within the confederacy. A chief in this group is called Loskenlakehte'kowa (los-gen-la-geh-te'-GO-wa), meaning "big, important man." A Big Man is chosen from the Mohawks, the Oneidas, the Onondagas, and the Cayugas. In accordance with Hiawatha's promise to the Senecas, this nation sends two Big Men to council meetings. Although Big Men have the right to attend league meetings, they have no voice in decision making. Names or titles of Big Men are vested in senior women of their clans. Successors are chosen by these women in the event of a Big Man's death. Big Men are installed in office with deer antler headdresses similar to those of confederacy councillors.

Big Men have the responsibility of planning and conducting military actions against foreign nations. Because of this duty, the founders did not allow Big Men to vote in confederacy decisions. The founders wisely were concerned that the Big Men might speak too loudly in favor of going to war. Hiawatha and the Peacemaker wanted peace, not war, to be the primary goal of the confederacy. Big Men also carry messages or announcements between confederacy chiefs. Finally, if any individual in a member nation wants to convey messages or opinions to confederacy chiefs meeting in council, he or she does so through the Big Man of his or her nation. As the founding charter states: "It shall ever be the duty of Big Men to lay the cases, questions, and propositions of the people before the Confederate Council."

Warfare among the Five Nations is outlawed by basic principles of confederation. According to the league's constitution, if conflicts erupt between the confederacy and any foreign nation, that nation is approached and invited to council. Leaders of the foreign group are asked to negotiate a settlement and to join with the Iroquois in the Great Peace. If a first council fails to resolve problems, Iroquois chiefs try twice more to peacefully solve the conflict. However, if all three councils fail, an Iroquois Big Man ceremonially declares war by holding out a bunch of white lake shells in his outstretched hand and letting them fall to the ground in front of the belligerent leaders.

If warfare erupts and the Iroquois are successful in defeating their enemy, peace is restored at the conclusion of war by confiscating all the enemy's weapons. Friendship is then established, and the former adversary is treated as a member of the Great Peace.

Each confederacy chief and Big Man has a subchief who is selected to assist him in his duties. The subchief may serve as a messenger or adviser. Subchiefs are ceremonially installed, but they do not have specific titles that are inherited.

In addition to confederacy chiefs, Big Men, and subchiefs, a fourth category of membership in the con-

For the Iroquois, dropping tobacco in the council fire, as seen in this illustration, symbolized peace. War, however, was declared by letting fall to the ground a handful of white lake shells.

feracy council consists of pine tree chiefs. These positions are granted to men who are not clan chiefs but who have special ability or commitment to the league's activities. They are active, distinguished members of their communities. Pine tree chiefs are elected by members of the confederacy. They are publicly proclaimed as a "pine tree sprung up for the nation." They may attend confederacy councils, but like Big Men, they do not participate in decision making. A man chosen as a pine tree chief retains that title for life. Additional chiefs can be named if their actions deserve the honor.

Confederacy chiefs and Big Men are selected for lifetime service. However, from time to time, a man installed in one of these positions might behave in a way that is deemed contrary to principles of the confederacy. Perhaps he fails to listen to advice and opinions offered by members of his clan or community. Perhaps he is disorderly or belligerent in his dealings with other councillors. Hiawatha and the Peacemaker understood that such behavior may occasionally occur. They included procedures in the Great Binding Law to deal with such problems. In these cases, the senior female noble of the chief's clan informs him that his actions are unacceptable and suggests reform. If he corrects his behavior, he remains in office. However, if he does not, he is given a second, sterner reprimand. A third and final warning can be given. If the chief continues to disregard the woman's words and ignores the sentiments of his community, he is impeached or deposed from office after the senior woman notifies the Big Man of her nation.

The confederacy allows all members of Iroquois communities to participate in discussions of important matters. Women and men in each village organize councils to consider problems and deliberate among themselves. As the confederacy charter states:

A pine tree chief displaying a wampum belt. Unlike confederacy chiefs, pine tree chiefs cannot participate in decision making.

The women of every clan of the Five Nations shall have a Council Fire ever burning in readiness for a council of the clan. When in their opinion it seems necessary for the interest of the people they shall hold a council and their decision and recommendation shall be introduced before the Council of Chiefs by the Big Man for its consideration.

A local council of men in each village was given similar instructions. Their opinions also are conveyed to league councillors by Big Men.

In this formulation of duties and rights, local concerns and the opinions of Iroquois villagers have a prominent place within the structure and functioning of the confederacy. The league was not envisioned as an organization external to or divorced from the people. It is a system aimed at satisfying the aspirations of all its members.

The rules of the Great Binding Law covered issues of membership, roles of chosen leaders, procedures for succession, and rights of local people. In addition, Hiawatha and the Peacemaker knew that social or political institutions should be flexible and allow for change. As the confederacy was likened to a communal longhouse, an addition to procedures and regulations is called a "new beam." If a change is adopted, it is considered "added to the rafters."

Hiawatha and the Peacemaker recognized the necessity of alleviating conflicts of all kinds that might erupt between individuals. The nations agreed to abandon warfare among themselves. In addition, the founders knew that conflicts sometimes were caused by competition over resources. Therefore, the Peacemaker proclaimed:

> We have still one matter left to be considered and that is with reference to the hunting grounds of our people from which they derive their living. We shall now do this: We shall only have one bowl in which will be placed one beaver's tail and we shall all have coequal right to it, and there shall be no knife in it, for if there be a knife in it, there would be danger that it might cut some one and blood would thereby be shed.

In other words, the Peacemaker's speech symbolically refers to the need to share resources without competition. The Iroquois shall eat from one common bowl and shall respect each other's rights and needs for land and food.

The Great Binding Law originated among the Iroquois, but provision was made to incorporate other groups. The charter of the league states: "If any person or nation outside the Five Nations shall obey the laws of the Great

Peace and make known their disposition to the Confederacy, they may trace the Great White Roots to the Tree and if their minds are clean and they are obedient and promise to obey the wishes of the Confederate Council, they shall be welcomed to take shelter beneath the Tree of the Long Leaves." This opportunity for others to join the league allowed neighbors and former enemies to live in peace.

The confederacy was an outgrowth of age-old Iroquois traditions for dealing with community problems and for reaching community consensus. Its wise founders, Hiawatha and the Peacemaker, understood the value of Iroquois customs. They recognized the strength that comes from balance and harmony. It is not necessary that all people begin with identical opinions, but they should be willing to listen to each other's views. Individuals should not be compelled to think or act contrary to their own wishes. Yet each person must also recognize the importance of group harmony. Everyone should be willing to compromise in order to achieve a communal goal.

Bowl with corn cakes. This "common bowl" signified, for the Iroquois, their need to share resources equally if they were to avoid conflict.

As an example of how these principles are put into practice, we can recall Hiawatha's negotiations in founding the confederacy. He used skillful diplomacy in winning over the obstinate and belligerent Thadodaho. He offered concessions to enhance Thadodaho's public stature by making him "first among equals." But Hiawatha first pressured Thadodaho by journeying to meet him with the combined strength of Mohawk, Oneida, Cayuga, and other Onondaga leaders. Even Thadodaho's stubbornness had to give way in the face of traditional community norms. In the end, he realized that he could not, and should not, attempt to thwart the people's will.

The confederacy is also linked to Iroquois culture through the kinship groups that form the bedrock of

Iroquois society. Senior women select chiefs who represent their clans. These women keep an ever-watchful eye on league proceedings and on the behavior of the chiefs who represent them. Clanswomen ensure the continuity of the confederacy just as they safeguard the continuity and well-being of their families.

From the beginning, the confederacy was responsive to the needs and wishes of local communities. Women and men in the villages gave advice to confederacy chiefs and Big Men. They expressed their opinions concerning matters before the council. They also voiced their approval or disapproval of decisions taken by the league. The chiefs, and the confederacy that they managed, were never separated from the people whose interests they pledged to serve. After all the procedures and principles of the Great Binding Law were set forth by Hiawatha and the Peacemaker and when they were accepted and adopted by the members, the Peacemaker announced:

> I will now leave all matters in the hands of your chiefs and you are to work and carry out the principles for the welfare of your people. I now place the power in your hands and to add to the rules and regulations whenever necessary. Each of you chiefs must never seriously disagree among yourselves. You are all of equal standing and of equal power.

In order to ensure that confederacy chiefs not pay attention to insults or gossip that might anger them and result in conflicts, the Peacemaker stated: "Your skin shall be of the thickness of seven spreads of the hands so that no matter how sharp a cutting instrument may be used it will not penetrate the thickness of your skin. You chiefs shall always be guided by the Good Tidings of Peace and Power."

With this symbolic language, the Peacemaker warned the chiefs not to be easily injured by harsh words or malicious gossip. Such rancor often led to conflicts and feuds in the days before Hiawatha and the Peacemaker undertook their mission of peace. The Peacemaker delivered his final hopes for the future:

> I charge you to cultivate the good feeling of friendship, love, and honor amongst yourselves. I have now fulfilled my duty in assisting you in the establishment and organization of this great confederacy, and if this confederation is carefully guarded it shall continue and endure from generation to generation and as long as the sun shines. Now I shall be seen no more and I go whither none can follow me. I shall now go home, conceal and cover myself with bark and there shall none other be called by my name.

The Peacemaker sailing away in a white-stone canoe. According to Iroquois legend, when the Peacemaker's work was done, he paddled toward the western setting sun and was never seen again.

In accordance with the Peacemaker's wishes, no successor to his name is ever chosen. Before departing, the Peacemaker gave one final warning: "And when it shall come to pass that the chiefs cannot agree, when they continually throw ashes at one another, the people will go astray, then the people's heads will roll."

But the Peacemaker told the council that if such conflicts occur, if the confederacy be threatened with discord and failure: "Call my name in the bushes and I will stand here once again."

And with that statement, according to traditional narratives, the Peacemaker left the council meeting and walked to the southern shore of Onondaga Lake. He then embarked in a canoe made of white stone and paddled toward the western setting sun. The Peacemaker disappeared from view and was never seen again. It is said that his grave, covered with hemlock boughs, is located on the far side of the lake.

Hiawatha remained among the councillors. He led them back to the council longhouse and said to them: "Let us now make one mind in which all the nations of the world shall be contained. We will have but one head, one soul, and but one tongue will be in us. And there shall be but one kind of blood."

Hiawatha returned to his adopted Mohawk home. He remained a respected chief of the Mohawks. His advice and wisdom were sought by many. Some tell that he lived a long life and died an elderly, honored man. Others say that Hiawatha eventually made his farewell to the Iroquois, walked to the shores of Lake Champlain, embarked in a white birch canoe, and disappeared. Hiawatha's wisdom and his hopes for peace and harmony are transmitted throughout the generations in countless repetitions of narratives of his deeds and his lasting vision.

5

ⱽ ⱽ ⱽ

RITUALS OF THE
CONFEDERACY

As ordained by Hiawatha and the Peacemaker, the roots of the Iroquois Confederacy were firmly embedded in traditional Iroquois culture. Another web of connections links the confederacy to the belief systems of the Iroquois people. Rituals and religious beliefs are intertwined with confederacy functions just as they are intertwined with daily life. One segment of the three-part message the Peacemaker first spoke of to Jikonsahseh was the word *Power*, which means both "authority of law and custom" and "religion and ritual." Among Iroquois peoples, religion and ritual were not separated from everyday experience. They provided explanations for all occurrences and gave meaning and direction to all actions.

The founders of the confederacy recognized the importance of ritual in unifying members of the community. Some of the rituals that were incorporated into procedures of the confederacy were derived from traditional Iroquois practices. Others were newly created by the founders and have since become part of Iroquois culture.

Confederacy meetings are opened and closed with ceremonial speeches, which traditionally were a part of all rituals. Thanksgiving addresses to the natural and

An Onondaga host greets chiefs at the start of a council meeting. One of the concessions offered by Hiawatha to Thadodaho in order to entice him to join the confederacy was that the Onondagas would have the privilege of opening councils.

supernatural worlds were recited in gratitude for the earth, sky, and all living creatures. The confederacy's charter states that all council meetings must begin with greetings by the Onondaga hosts, welcoming and thanking the chiefs for their attendance. In accordance with traditional Iroquois rituals, thanks are then offered to creatures and forces of the universe in a set order, beginning with those entities closest to the earth and proceeding skyward:

> The Onondaga chiefs shall offer thanks to the earth where people dwell, to the streams of water, the pools, the springs and the lakes, to the maize and the fruits, to the medicinal herbs and trees, to the forest trees for their usefulness, to the animals that serve as food and give their pelts for clothing, to the great winds and the lesser winds, to the Thunderers, to the Sun, to the Moon, to the messengers of the Creator, and to the Great Creator who dwells in the heavens above, who gives all the things useful to people, and who is the source and the ruler of health and life.

This ancient Iroquois speech of thanksgiving is incorporated into confederacy councils. It expresses a basic Iroquois view of the world—that all living creatures and all forces of nature are united in a harmonious, balanced relationship. All share what they have, giving good things to one another. The earth provides a place for all life to exist. The streams, lakes, and springs provide drinking water and a means of transportation. Wild and cultivated plants are the source of foods and medicines that ensure people's survival. Animals allow themselves to be caught and eaten. The winds and thunder bring air and rain necessary for growth and survival. The sun and moon nurture and watch over the earth. And finally, spirit beings and the creator are sources of power, knowledge, and protection. In recognition of the bounty of the universe and its gifts, people are obliged to express their gratitude in rituals of thanksgiving. These messages are conveyed to spirits and forces guiding and sustaining the universe. They express the continual bond and inter-dependence between people and other forms of life. They also signify the harmony and balance that nurtures and safeguards the existence of all.

Much of the speech referring to the confederacy—and the style of speaking used in council deliberations—is

A significant view of the Iroquois—and one that is expressed in confederacy rituals—is that all living beings and the forces of nature are united in a balanced and harmonious relationship.

rich in metaphor, symbolic references, and imagery. Gifted orators such as Hiawatha are able to use elaborate imagery in order to convey their ideas. Such speaking styles create a sense of dignity and power. They give even the most ordinary event an aura of ritual.

The image of the Longhouse is a recurring symbol for the confederacy. Its sturdy structure represents the strength of the league. The families of nations within the confederacy's Longhouse are connected to the matrilineal families dwelling in their communal lodges. And the rules of the Great Binding Law are rafters in the Longhouse. They support and safeguard the unified nations. Rafters can be extended and added to when the need arises in order to support the basic structure of unity.

The warmth from the central hearth of the confederacy's Longhouse nurtures the unity of the Five Nations just as heat from cooking fires sustains human existence. The central council fire at the Onondaga village is kindled by firebrands from council hearths at each of the Five Nations. This act symbolizes the merging of national and local interests into one common purpose.

The Peacemaker proclaimed that chestnut wood should never be used in council fires because when chestnut wood burns it throws out sparks. Such sparks would cause a disturbance and symbolically represent discord among chiefs.

Kindling of the council fire symbolizes harmony among the nations. In contrast, extinguishing the fire and covering up the ashes symbolize the inability of league chiefs to reach consensus. The imagery of fires and hearths also appears in references to foreign nations. When foreigners are brought into the confederation, "a council fire for the Great Law will be kindled" for them.

Another symbol of unity among the Five Nations is a bundle of five arrows, which are tied tightly together

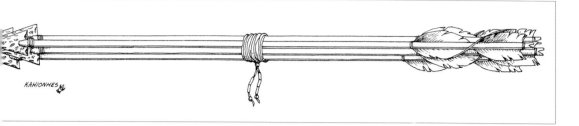

KAHIONHES

Five bound arrows is yet
another symbol of the unity of
the original Five Nations of
the Iroquois League.

with strong deer sinew. The Peacemaker told the assembly of chiefs:

> We shall now combine our individual power into one great
> power which is this confederacy and we shall symbolize the
> union of these powers by each Nation contributing one
> arrow, which we shall tie up together in a bundle which,
> when it is made and completely tied together, no one can
> bend or break. This bundle of arrows signifies that all the
> chiefs and all the men and all the women of the Confederacy have become united as one person.

The Great Tree of Peace is a central symbol of the confederation. The Peacemaker ceremonially planted this enormous pine tree at the Onondaga village, which is the geographic center of Iroquois territory. The White Roots of Peace secure the tree to the earth. They spread out in cardinal directions, leading to distant places. The branches and long leaves protect the people who take shelter under the tree. The Peacemaker declared:

> The shadow of the tree will be pleasant and beautiful.
> Never again shall people walk in fear. All the peoples of
> the world will dwell there in peace and tranquility, for all
> will deposit their minds there. We will have one head, one
> tongue, and one blood in our bodies.

The Tree of Confederation grows ever taller as more nations are brought in under its protection. Its White Roots of Peace were uprooted once in order to bury weapons of war formerly used by the Five Nations against each other. With the act of replanting the roots, the confederacy was firmly established. The roots extend to all nations. As others desire to join the league, they follow the roots to their source at the Great Tree of Peace. These nations are then welcomed to the shade and security provided by the long leaves. This poetic and majestic image is also found in the concept of the pine tree chiefs, who are "sprung up for the nation." Finally, it recurs in the ceremony for installing new confederacy chiefs. In rituals of installation, chiefs are "raised up" for the league just as a tree or log is raised up when building a house.

The central figure of Chief Thadodaho is also given ceremonial and symbolic functions. Thadodaho announces meetings, opens councils, and declares league decisions. In addition, the Peacemaker gave Thadodaho an eagle wing and a long pole to protect the proceedings. The Peacemaker told him: "You, Thadodaho, shall faithfully keep the space about the Council Fire clean and you shall allow neither dust nor dirt to accumulate. I lay a Long Wing before you as a broom. As a weapon against a crawling creature I lay a staff with you so that you may thrust it away from the Council Fire."

This speech symbolically refers to Thadodaho's responsibility to make sure that meetings are orderly and that only relevant topics are discussed. Thadodaho must clear away dust and dirt, which cover the clarity of discussion. He must eliminate "crawling creatures," which distract one's attention. The Peacemaker further explained the imagery of insects to signify danger:

> Whenever you see any creeping thing which might have a tendency to harm our grandchildren or see a thing creeping toward the Great Peace, then you shall take this rod and pry it away, and if you and your colleagues fail to pry the creeping, evil thing out, you shall then call out loudly that all the Confederate Nations may hear and they will come immediately to your assistance.

In other words, if discord arises in Iroquois villages or among the Iroquois nations or if danger approaches from foreign places, all confederate nations must rally to the call to reestablish unity or to defend themselves against external dangers.

The meanings and functions of wampum are interwoven with the activities of the confederacy. Wampum was originated by Hiawatha from the white and purple shells he found at the bottom of the lake and on surrounding shorelines. The Peacemaker later used the strings of shells to condole Hiawatha, clearing his body, mind, and spirit as the shells symbolically became words of comfort. This powerful imagery is incorporated into rituals of condolence that occur upon the death of any Iroquois.

Although the earliest sources of wampum were the shells of lake snails, the Iroquois later obtained wampum through trade with other Indians living in present-day Long Island, New York, and coastal New Jersey. These people gathered clam shells and conch shells, which they cut into small pieces. They then fashioned beads of white and purple shell. Wampum beads became a much-desired trade item that the Iroquois secured in enormous numbers. Wampum is used to symbolically represent words and messages of many types. Wampum beads are either strung together or woven into belts. Different patterns of white and purple shells represent different messages. A belt of all-white wampum symbolizes peace, whereas one of purple or dark wampum means war. In establishing the confederacy, the Peacemaker spread before the Onondaga Fire-keepers a Great White Wampum Belt of Peace to signify the harmony and beauty of peaceful existence. The Fire-keepers are charged with protecting its purity.

Five strands of white wampum tied together are another symbol of the Five Nations united in peace. At

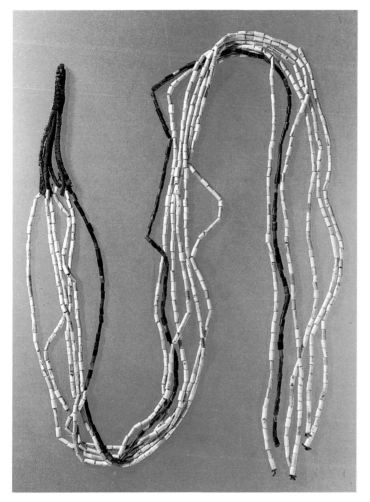

Strings of shell beads, known as wampum, were originated by Hiawatha. The white strings represent the Five Nations, and the purple string represents peoples who would unite in peace with the league.

the beginning of a council session, the speaker who opens the meeting holds the strings of wampum in his hand while he delivers the welcoming address. When he is finished, he attaches them to a pole erected near the council fire to signify that the council is in session.

The confederacy's charter describes the Wampum Belt of Confederation, also referred to as the Hiawatha Belt. It is "a broad dark belt of wampum of thirty-eight rows, having a white heart in the center, on either side of which are two white squares all connected with the heart by white rows of beads." It is the emblem of the unity of the Five Nations. The central heart represents the Onondaga nation. The four white squares on the sides represent the other four Iroquois nations. Those on the left are Mohawk and Oneida emblems; those on the right signify the Cayugas and Senecas.

The central heart in the Hiawatha Belt has several additional meanings. According to the confederacy's constitution, "It means that the heart of the Five Nations is single in its loyalty to the Great Peace, that the Great Peace is lodged in the heart or center (Onondaga territory), and that the Council Fire is to burn there for the Five Nations." The white heart and white squares symbolize peace and signify that "no evil or jealous thoughts shall creep into the minds of the Chiefs in council under the Great Peace. White, the emblem of peace, love, charity, and equity surrounds and guards the Five Nations."

When confederacy councils end their deliberations and reach consensus, their decisions are "read into" strings or belts of wampum. These belts are kept by an Onondaga chief belonging to the Wolf Clan. He is responsible for safeguarding the records of council meetings.

When treaties were negotiated with foreign nations (including later agreements between the Iroquois and governments of European countries, the United States, and Canada), wampum belts were made to preserve the accords. Patterns of wampum serve as mnemonic (memory) devices that enable people to recall and recount significant events and agreements.

Traditional stories of the Iroquois relate that after the league's foundation and the Peacemaker's departure, Hiawatha sent out emissaries to many distant Indian peoples. Messengers went to the Hurons, Petuns, and Ottawas in the north; the Delawares and Cherokees to the south; and the Shawnees, Miamis, and Sacs to the west. They told of the Great Peace, secured agreements with many of these groups, and brought back wampum belts to signify their treaties.

From time to time, confederacy speakers display and read wampum belts that record laws of the confederacy or important events. The person who reads the belts is given a special mat made of wild hemp fibers to sit upon. The mat is used only once because the occasion of recounting laws and agreements is so solemn that it is considered unsuitable to reuse the mat as though it were an ordinary household object.

Wampum also functioned as symbolic tribute. It was paid by groups who had been defeated in war. Vanquished peoples were required to give quantities of wampum strings to Mohawk emissaries in recognition of their defeat and conciliation to peace.

Another use of wampum within Iroquois communities was as a token of atonement after acts of murder. Prior to Hiawatha's era, when murders occurred between villagers, blood feuds often erupted and continued for many years, sometimes for generations. Hiawatha's vision of peace sought to defuse discord arising in such circumstances. He instituted the custom of payment in wampum from the family of a murderer to that of the victim. Fines were set at rates that were determined by the gender of the murderer and the victim. A man's life was valued at 10 strings of wampum, whereas a woman's was set at 20 strings. A woman's life was deemed more valuable because she made possible the continuity of generations. In the event of a woman's murder, not only was her own life lost to the community but also those of children she might have borne. According to Iroquois custom, if a man killed another man, his family offered the victim's family a tribute of 20 strings of wampum. This fine included 10 strings for the man who was killed and 10 for the murderer. (Murderers had to pay for their own lives because they were considered useless to their community.) If a man killed a woman, his family gave 30 strings— 20 for her life and 10 for his own. If a woman committed murder, her family gave 30 strings to a male victim's kin and 40 to relatives of a female victim.

Many recurring symbols and images are woven into specific rituals performed within the confederacy. A most solemn and complex cycle of ceremonies occurs after the death of a league chief. These "condolence councils" express the sorrow of bereaved nations, the comfort extended by other nations, and the unity and continuity of the confederacy. They take place in autumn or winter following a chief's death. They never occur in spring or summer because these seasons are times when all people, other creatures, and forces of nature are concerned with growth and life. The Iroquois believe that rituals centered around death interfere with the life-giving forces of the planting and growing seasons.

The Hiawatha Belt, or Wampum Belt of Confederation. The pine tree in the middle signifies the league. The belt was damaged and is now incomplete.

Condolence councils mourn the death of a chief but they also are occasions for "raising up" his successor. They are performed for confederacy chiefs, Big Men, and their subchiefs as well. When a chief dies, a member of his nation, but not of his clan, travels to the other nations, carrying strings of black wampum, signifying death. As the messenger runs on his journeys, he utters a sad wail at frequent intervals. When he arrives in a village, he tells the inhabitants of the chief's death. He gives them a string of wampum, saying: "Here is the testimony, you have heard the message." Chiefs from this village then send runners to all the other nations to transmit the sad news.

When the time comes for condoling the bereaved, all chiefs, Big Men, and senior women from the Five Nations participate. The nations are divided into two groups, the "mourners" and the "clear minded," in accordance with their moiety arrangement. The mourning nations consist of the nation whose chief has died and the other nations in its moiety. The clear-minded group consists of nations in the opposite moiety. Thus, if a Mohawk chief has died, the mourning group includes the Mohawks, the Onondagas, and the Senecas; the Oneidas and the Cayugas are the clear minded. This division affects the ceremonial roles that people perform at condolences.

The Peacemaker proclaimed that after a chief's death, people of clear-minded nations should proceed to the home village of the chief's nation to condole them. The mourners assemble around a fire in a clearing outside their village and await the travelers. Members of the visiting nations approach the fire and are then greeted by the mourners. Greetings express thanks for the long journey and safe arrival of the travelers.

Condoling begins when the clear-minded chant a Hymn of Peace to the mourners. Later, a clear-minded

Wampum strings were also used by the Iroquois as a token of payment. When wampum was used to atone for a killing, a man's life was valued at 10 strings, whereas a woman's was valued at 20 strings.

chief recites the three words or comforting messages that Hiawatha first spoke to the strings of shells in his lament after his daughters' deaths. These words remove mist and obstructions from the mourners' eyes, ears, and throat and restore them to clear sight, hearing, and speech. Their bodies are restored to health and vigor. Their minds are made straight and full of courage.

After the clear-minded speaker ends condoling, the whole assembly proceeds to the longhouse of the mourners. Along the way, a singer from among the clear-minded recites a chant given by the Peacemaker, which is called the Roll Call of Chiefs. It lists the names of each of the 50 confederacy chiefs. Names of chiefs are listed by nation and by clan within each nation. After each name is chanted, the singer proclaims:

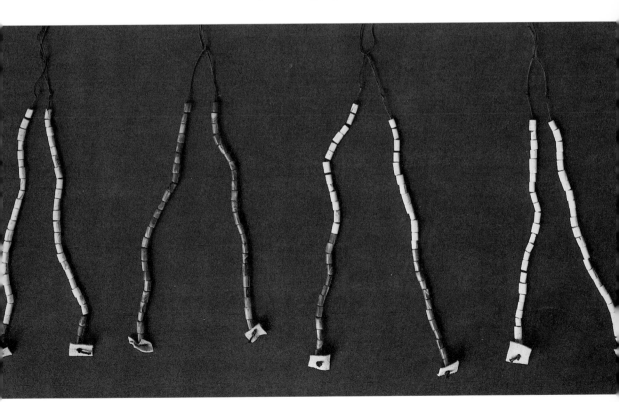

Continue to listen, you who were a founder.

After naming a set of clan members within a nation, the singer repeats the refrain:

> This was the roll of you,
> You that joined in the work,
> You who completed the work,
> The Great League.

Shouts of "Hai Hai" are made by others in the assembly. These sounds are believed to be the cry of souls. Upon hearing the shouts, the souls are themselves consoled.

Next, a speaker from the clear minded continues condoling the mourners by repeating the words of Hiawatha's comforting speech. Afterward, a member of the mourning group thanks their guests for removing each "burden" and restoring them to health and clarity. At the end of this recitation, a clear-minded speaker exclaims:

> Now show me the man.

When these words are spoken, the senior woman of the deceased chief's clan presents the candidate to be installed or "raised up" in the former chief's place. The new chief is given his title by the Big Man of his nation. The headdress of deer antlers is placed on his head, endowing him with the emblem of office. Finally, the new chief is told of his duties and responsibilities as a member of the confederacy council.

A new chief is especially advised to think of the welfare of the young generations and those yet to be born:

> Devote special care to the children who run to and fro, to
> the children who still creep and crawl, to the children
> whose bodies are still made fast to cradleboards, and to
> those unborn children who, with faces turned this way, are
> on their way here.

A dehorning ceremony. If a chief has to be deposed, he is "dehorned," a reference to his losing his deer antler head-dress.

Most chiefs pay careful attention to these words and instructions and follow the path of peace. But occasionally a chief's actions require that he be removed from office. When a chief is deposed because he has failed to heed advice and warnings to correct unsuitable behavior, a ceremony of "dehorning" is performed. This rite takes its name from reference to the headdress of deer antler horns that symbolizes a chief's office. The headdress is removed from the errant chief by the Big Man of his nation. The Big Man makes the following proclamation:

> So you disregard and set at naught the warnings of your women relatives. So you fling the warnings over your shoulder to cast them behind you. Behold the brightness of the Sun and in the brightness of the Sun's light I depose you of your title and remove the sacred emblem of your Chief's title. . . . I now depose you and return the antlers to the women whose heritage they are.

In a final rebuke, the Big Man continues to admonish the deposed chief: "You are no longer Chief. You shall now go your way alone, the rest of the people of the Confederacy will not go with you, for we know not the kind of mind that possesses you. . . . You shall never be restored to the position which you once occupied."

These words are harsh. They express the severe condemnation felt toward people who ignore the sentiments of their family and community. According to Iroquois ethics, people should be cooperative, generous, and helpful to others. They should be mindful of others' rights and take care not to offend. Conformity to community standards does not mean a lack of individual freedom. It recognizes that communal well-being and harmony are valued human goals. People entrusted with valued positions should be especially cooperative. They should not use their status to violate the rights or sentiments of members of their families, villages, or nations.

All of these various rituals and the recitation of prayers and chants maintain the stability and continuity of the confederacy. Iroquois ethical values and the hope of people for peace and harmony are repeated countless times. These messages express and reinforce people's view of the kind of world in which they live. Perhaps more important, they also express people's view of the type of world in which they wish to exist.

A condolence ceremony. When a chief dies, the confederacy is divided into two groups—the "clear minded" (who do the condoling) and the "mourners."

6

▽ ▽ ▽

THE POWER OF THE CONFEDERACY

After the confederacy was firmly established, Hiawatha sent emissaries to many nearby and distant peoples to spread the news of the Great Peace. He invited these nations to follow the White Roots to the Tree of Long Leaves and to take shelter under its tranquil branches. Hiawatha knew that all people would prosper if they lived in peace with their neighbors. Hiawatha's messengers returned with wampum belts signifying assent from numerous nations.

From the Shawnees they brought the message: "We have put the mind and thought of our great company of warriors in this belt."

From the Delawares: "It is good. Here we have put our voice and here we have cast our mind."

From the Algonquins: "We accept the law single-minded. We cast our minds as one upon this belt. As a single body we cast our minds."

From the Miamis: "We verily have seen the law. We place our entire mind in this belt where we will leave it."

Similar messages of gratitude and acceptance were given by peoples to the north, the west, and the south.

Some pledged to help spread the Great Peace even farther by carrying its words to more distant places.

It is not known whether the Great Peace lasted among groups outside the Five Nations during Hiawatha's lifetime. However, by the 17th century, the people of the Longhouse were sometimes engaged in conflicts with their neighbors. It is also unclear how severe these struggles were before the arrival of Europeans on North American shores. In any case, violence certainly intensified after European contact. Indeed, the worsening of intertribal warfare in the Northeast and in all of North America was a direct result of actions and policies of Europeans.

By the beginning of the 17th century, the Iroquois had few alliances with other Indian peoples. They relied on the skills of their astute diplomats to dominate the politics of the Northeast. They relied as well on the deeds of their warriors to maintain and spread their control. Through this powerful combination of diplomacy and force, the Iroquois Confederacy influenced the economies of many

A beaver, sculpted from moose antler by Stanley Hill in 1981. For the Iroquois, this furry creature was an important clan symbol; for 17th-century Europeans, however, beaver pelts made fashionable hats and collars.

Indian and European communities. In addition, the Iroquois eventually influenced conditions of war and peace in the entire region.

In order to understand the role of the Iroquois in North American history, it is necessary to consider the changes brought about by European colonization. Traders came from Holland, Great Britain, and France, bringing many goods that they wanted to trade with the Indians. In exchange, they wanted Native Americans in the Northeast to supply them with beaver skins to satisfy the desires of European consumers. In 17th-century Europe, hats and collars made of beaver were much in fashion.

At first, it seemed as though there were an endless supply of beavers in the Northeast. However, these animals soon dwindled to a very few. The rapid decline in their population resulted from overkill. Before European contact, the Indians had always been careful not to kill too many beavers. Whenever they trapped a group of animals, they made sure to leave some of them alive so that they would survive to reproduce. Such conservation measures, though, disappeared as European demand for the pelts increased.

The Iroquois and other Native American groups obtained many items from Europeans that made their life more comfortable. Most important were objects made of metal, such as iron knives, kettles, pots, spoons, scissors, needles, and nails. Before European contact, the Indians spent many hours making implements out of animal bone, stone, wood, or clay. Such implements not only took a long time to make, but they also broke, burned, or decayed quite easily. Therefore, the Indians preferred European goods because they were more durable. In addition, Native Americans obtained from European traders heavy woolen cloth, which they made into cloaks for wear during rainy or cold weather.

Soon, objects that were first thought of as novelties and luxuries became necessities of life. However, there was a disadvantage in becoming too dependent on trade. In order to obtain European products, the Indians were compelled to trap beavers in enormous numbers to trade for the items that they wanted. As the Indians became more involved in trade, they also began to compete with each other for the dwindling supply of beavers remaining in the Northeast. This caused widespread intertribal conflicts in the region.

To complicate matters even further, the Europeans were at war with each other. Holland, Great Britain, and France were economic and political rivals both in Europe and in North America. They each tried to forge alliances with various Indian peoples in order to dominate trade. Whenever military conflict erupted among Europeans, they also tried to get their Indian trading allies to help them in warfare against their enemies. In a very short time, the Iroquois and other Native American groups in the Northeast were entangled in deadly wars, sometimes against Europeans, sometimes against each other.

The Iroquois Confederacy quickly established a decisive position for itself in this arena. In the early 17th century, the Iroquois concluded treaties of friendship with Dutch merchants who had built a trading post at Fort Orange on the Hudson River. When the British defeated the Dutch in 1664, they established control over Fort Orange, renaming it Albany. In the same year, the confederacy negotiated an economic and military alliance with the British. Although this alliance had its difficulties, it lasted until the American Revolution, which began in 1776.

The Iroquois faced a very serious problem, however. Beavers were never as abundant in Iroquois territory as in the more northerly regions. In fewer than 30 years of

Besides their desire for European-made implements, Native Americans also grew to enjoy the more durable garments that could be made from European cloth.

heavy trapping, these animals were nearly extinct in the East. The Iroquois had to choose between two alternatives. The first was to completely abandon trading for European goods. This was unacceptable to most Iroquois because it would mean giving up the metal utensils, cloth, and other products upon which the Indians had come to rely. The second choice was to trade indirectly by obtaining fur from other Indians who still had plenty of beavers in their territory. The Iroquois preferred this option.

However, because other peoples also wanted to trade with the Europeans, the Iroquois were compelled to obtain furs by a combination of diplomacy and force. In response to the Europeans' need for fur, bitter intertribal struggles over access to furs and to trading routes ensued, lasting for nearly two centuries.

The Iroquois were geographically well situated and used their location to their advantage. To the east, the

Mohawk nation controlled the Hudson and Mohawk rivers leading to Fort Orange. In the north, the Onondagas were near eastern Lake Ontario, which emptied into the St. Lawrence River. These waterways led to French trading posts at Montreal and Quebec. In the west, the Senecas were located next to lands of other nations, such as the Hurons, Neutrals, and Eries, all of whom had large supplies of beaver in their territory.

The confederacy used two approaches to gain control of trade: peace and war. League leaders used negotiation as one method of establishing control. They wanted to extend the Great White Roots far and wide, bringing all nations under the protection of the Tree of Long Leaves.

The Iroquois hoped to become intermediaries in trade networks between Native Americans and Europeans.

As part of the tanning process, beaver skin was stretched out on a circular frame and dried in the sun, as shown in this illustration.

They would obtain furs from northern or western peoples and trade them to Europeans for goods. Then they would receive more furs from other Indians in exchange for some of the trade objects. Some Indian groups agreed to this arrangement, possibly because it saved them from having to make long, difficult journeys to British or French trading posts. But many peoples preferred to deal directly with the merchants because they were then able to keep all of the trade goods given for the furs. Iroquois go-betweens naturally kept some of the goods for themselves.

When diplomacy failed to achieve peaceful results, armed conflict took its place. Members of the confederacy organized raids against other Indian groups in order to force them to agree to Iroquois economic control. Several Indian peoples decided to leave their homelands because of the frequent warfare. By the middle of the 17th century, many people among the Hurons, Eries, and Neutrals had fled to the west. Many others agreed to live among the Iroquois. These immigrants supplemented confederacy villages, which were losing members because of the wars.

It therefore happened that the prophecy foretold by the messenger to the Peacemaker's mother did come to pass. The messenger had said that the Peacemaker would indirectly cause the destruction of the Huron (Wendat) people. As a result of the Peacemaker's plan for unity among the Five Nations, the Iroquois were able to amass the strength to defeat the Hurons. In 1649, after years of Iroquois raids, the Hurons dispersed, traveling to the west and east.

As other Indians abandoned their traditional homelands, the Iroquois were able to expand their own hunting territory into these areas. They could then obtain a greater supply of beavers for trade with the Europeans.

The British were often directly involved in Indian conflicts. They participated by urging their Iroquois allies to attack Indian allies of the French. These groups included the Ottawas, Hurons, and Algonquins.

For their part, the French tried to win the Iroquois over to their side. They hoped to break the Iroquois alliance with the British. Although the Iroquois never completely trusted the French, they were also distrustful of British promises. The British often urged the Iroquois to wage war against the French but rarely sent many English soldiers to help in these battles. They did very little to help protect Iroquois villages from French attacks. Therefore, in order to safeguard their own position, Iroquois diplomats attempted to secure friendship and peace agreements with the French. Such accords did not last long.

To compound the difficulties that the Iroquois encountered, by the early 18th century, British colonists moved farther and farther into Iroquois territory. As their numbers increased, so did their appetite for land. Leaders of the confederacy continually urged British officials to respect their rights to land and safety. Although the officials made many promises, they were apt to ignore settlers' incursions into Iroquois territory.

British colonial expansion in the Southeast also affected the Iroquois Confederacy. An Indian group known as the Tuscaroras had settled in present-day Virginia and North Carolina long before the arrival of the Europeans in North America. The Tuscaroras are related to the Iroquois by language, history, and culture. After British settlement in the Southeast resulted in decades of conflict, the Tuscaroras sent messengers to the confederacy in the early 18th century. They asked to be allowed to follow the Great White Roots to the Great Tree of Peace. In 1722, the Tuscaroras were taken in as the sixth nation in the Iroquois Confederacy. The Tuscaroras "added a frame

The French and their Indian allies attack an Iroquois fort in 1615. As Europeans battled each other for supremacy in North America in the early 18th century, the Indians were pushed into the conflict and were forced to take sides.

pole to the great framework" of the Longhouse. They sit in council meetings on the side of the Younger nations, along with the Oneidas and the Cayugas. However, no names were added to the council of the 50 confederacy chiefs. Therefore, Tuscarora representatives do not have official titles.

By the mid-18th century, the situation for the Iroquois in New York was worsening. Settlers from Great Britain, Holland, and Germany were entering their territory in ever-increasing numbers. Some Iroquois sold portions of their land to colonists. The Iroquois lost much additional acreage through fraudulent transactions and outright thefts. Few British officials did anything to protect Iroquois rights. However, one Briton of the period, Sir William Johnson, was trusted and respected by the Iroquois. Johnson began his career in the 1740s as a trader to the Iroquois and operated a successful business at his post, called Johnson Hall, located near present-day Johnstown, New York. Johnson was well liked by the Iroquois, in part because he treated them with respect. He spoke up on behalf of Iroquois interests and tried to defend their rights. Because of his good relations with the Iroquois, he was appointed commissioner to manage Indian affairs for the British colonial administration in New York. However, he had a falling-out with the New York Assembly over the cost of gifts he distributed at councils with the Iroquois. These donations were in accord with the Iroquois custom of exchanging presents on important public occasions. To the regret of Iroquois leaders, Johnson resigned his position in 1750.

Johnson continued to maintain good relations with the Iroquois. Another reason that the Iroquois liked him was that he adopted many of their customs when interacting with them. He often dressed in Indian clothing and took part in their rituals. On June 28, 1756, Johnson traveled to Onondaga to condole the death of an Iroquois chief. In his journals, Johnson described the proceedings as follows:

> About a mile from Onondaga, three Cayugas met us, and a halt was made of two hours, to settle the formalities of the condolence, agreeable to the ancient Custom of the Six Nations. Then I marched on at the Head of the Chiefs singing the condoling song which contains the names, laws, and customs of their renowned ancestors, and praying that their deceased brother might be blessed with happiness in his other state.

The influential Mohawk chief, Hendrick, spoke well of Johnson and expressed the opinion of all the Iroquois when he said: "He has large ears and heareth a great deal, and what he hears he tells us; he also has large eyes and sees a great way, and conceals nothing from us."

During this period, the French and Indian War erupted between Great Britain and France, lasting from 1754 to 1763. The Iroquois maintained their alliance with Great Britain. In fact, Iroquois military support for the British during the war played a decisive role in Britain's victory.

However, the Iroquois did not prosper as a result of their alliance. After the French were defeated, the British no longer had serious competition for Indian trade in New York. Therefore, they could ignore Iroquois interests even more than they had done before the war. In addition, as the British desired more and more Iroquois land, officials paid less attention to Iroquois claims against fraudulent practices of the colonists. The Iroquois signed many treaties with Great Britain in an attempt to secure borders for Indian land. Despite these agreements, incursions by settlers continued unabated.

During the years leading up to the American Revolution, British and American leaders tried to obtain pledges of support by the confederacy. The Americans feared that the Iroquois would fight on the side of Great Britain. However, they hoped to convince the Iroquois to remain neutral. In 1775, the Continental Congress sent an urgent message to the confederacy council:

> In our consultation we have judged it proper and necessary to send you this talk, as we are upon the same island, that you may be informed of the reasons of this great Council. . . . This is a family quarrel between us and old England. We desire you to remain at home, and not join on either side, but keep the hatchet buried deep.

In exchange for Iroquois neutrality, the Americans promised to supply the Indians with necessary items, such as utensils and woolen clothing.

Hendrick, an influential Mohawk chief, converted to Christianity and sided with the English against the French. He died in battle in 1755 at the age of 70.

British officials also made appeals to the confederacy. They reminded the Iroquois of the long-standing alliance between their peoples. In addition, they argued that if the American colonists were to be victorious and took control of the government, Iroquois lands would surely be taken.

Confederacy leaders held many councils to discuss this problem. Councillors were deeply divided over their allegiances. The Oneidas were strongest in support of the rebels. Most Mohawks, Senecas, and Onondagas wanted to maintain their British alliance. However, there were factions within each group favoring different sides. Many favored peaceful neutrality. The confederacy chiefs decided to follow the neutral path by not officially supporting either the British or the Americans. But the strain caused by disagreement among the nations shook the roots of the Great Tree of Peace. Failing to "roll their words into one bundle," the chiefs covered up the council fire at Onondaga in 1777. This act signaled the last days of the confederacy as a dominant political and military force in the Northeast.

Throughout the history of contact between the Iroquois and Europeans, many traders, officials, missionaries, and scholars marveled at the diplomatic skill of Iroquois leaders and the military prowess of Iroquois warriors. They marveled too at the institution of the confederacy itself, which welded their distinct nations into one common union, with "one heart, one mind, one soul, and one blood."

A French priest and scholar of the early 18th century, Pierre Charlevoix, wrote about the Iroquois councils that he attended. He commented:

Proceedings are carried on in these assemblies with a wisdom and coolness, and a knowledge of affairs, and I may add generally with a probity, which would have done honor to the senates of Athens or Rome in the most glorious days of those republics. Nothing is resolved upon with precipitation. Those violent passions, which have so much disgraced the politics even of Christians, have never prevailed amongst the Iroquois over the public good. All is performed with a dignity, an attention, and with a capacity equal to the most important affairs.

Europeans were especially impressed by the amazing abilities of the Iroquois people to remember the exact words of speeches and provisions of agreements. Iroquois methods of remembering and recalling speeches were described by Cadwallader Colden, a British surveyor general in New York in the mid-18th century:

> They commonly repeat over all that has been said to them, before they return any answer, and one may be surprised at the exactness of these repetitions. They take the following method to assist their memories: the Chief has a bundle of small sticks in his hand; as soon as the speaker has finished any one article of his speech, this Chief gives a stick to another Chief, who is particularly to remember that article; and so when another article is finished, he gives a stick to another to take care of that other, and so on.

Thayendanegea, or Joseph Brant, was a celebrated Mohawk leader who fought on the side of the British during the American Revolution. The confederacy could not reach a consensus as to which country the Iroquois should side with during the revolutionary war.

In this way, the exact wording of the whole treaty or agreement is recalled.

By using methods of recall, the Iroquois were able to transmit details of agreements for generations. As Benjamin Franklin noted in 1784: "They preserve traditions of stipulations in treaties 100 years back; which, when we compare with our writings, we always find exact."

Iroquois speakers also used wooden canes as aids to their memories. These canes were carved on both sides with pictographs to prompt speakers at condolence councils. Because of this use, they are often called Condolence Canes. One side has pictographs signifying sections of the condolence songs. The other side has carvings that represent each of the 50 confederacy chiefs. They are depicted in the order set for reciting the Roll Call of Chiefs at rituals for condoling and raising up the new chiefs.

Many European and American observers were also impressed with the poetic speech of Iroquois orators. Colden's history of the Iroquois provides many speeches of Indian leaders of the 17th and early 18th centuries that continued the poetic imagery used by Hiawatha and the Peacemaker centuries before. In 1684, Iroquois chiefs met with governors of the colonies of Virginia and Maryland in order to conclude a treaty of friendship. A Mohawk chief spoke for the Five Nations and said: "We now plant a Tree, whose tops will reach the Sun, and its Branches spread far abroad, so that it shall be seen afar off; and we shall shelter ourselves under it, and live in Peace."

At the signing of a treaty between the Iroquois and the colonies of Massachusetts and Connecticut in 1689, a Mohawk chief remarked: "We make fast the Roots of the Tree of Peace and Tranquility, which is planted in this place. Its Roots extended as far as the utmost of your Colonies. If the French should come to shake this Tree, we would feel it by the Motion of its Roots, which extend into our Country."

A few years later, an Iroquois chief assured the governor of New York of their continued allegiance by saying: "We assure you we will never separate from you. We still have one head, one blood, one soul, and one heart with you."

Iroquois leaders also used their skillful speech to criticize English and French officials who had failed to live up to their agreements. Thus, a confederacy chief admonished Colonel Benjamin Fletcher, a British official, at a conference in Albany in 1694:

Benjamin Franklin, one of the Founding Fathers of the United States, takes notes during an Iroquois council. Franklin admired the organized manner in which the confederacy functioned.

The Chain with the English has been enlarged and strengthened. The other colonies have thrust their Arms into this Chain but have given little or no assistance against the common Enemy (France). Our arms are stiff and tired with holding fast the Chain, whilst our Neighbors sit still and smoke at their ease. The Fat is melted from our Flesh, and has fallen on our Neighbors, who grow fat while we grow lean. They flourish while we decay.

Some Europeans and Americans admired the success of the confederacy. During the revolutionary war, when

American leaders were struggling to establish their own form of government, Benjamin Franklin wrote of the Iroquois:

> It would be a strange thing if six nations of [Indians] should be capable of forming a scheme for such a union and be able to execute it in such a manner that it has subsisted for ages and appears indissoluble; and yet that a like union should be impractible for ten or a dozen English colonies to whom it is more necessary and who cannot be supposed to want an equal understanding of their interests.

Although Franklin's words reveal some of the arrogance with which many people of his day viewed non-European cultures, they do express an appreciation of Iroquois accomplishments.

Hiawatha and the Peacemaker organized the Iroquois nations into a united confederacy as a response to the conditions of their times. They understood the need to establish peace among themselves in order to withstand dangers from external enemies. They also knew that their strength lay in unity and harmony. The Iroquois people took hold of this great idea and followed the White Roots of Peace to the Tree of Long Leaves because they realized that under that tree were the hopes of their own survival.

7

HIAWATHA'S LEGACY

Since the later years of the 18th century, the Iroquois people have experienced enormous changes in their lives. In the years during and after the American Revolution, many Iroquois abandoned their villages in New York and resettled in several communities in Canada. Even though most Iroquois did not actively participate in the war, they were attacked in New York by American settlers who wanted their land. As a final blow, toward the end of the war, George Washington sent James Clinton and John Sullivan on a campaign to destroy the remaining villages of the Onondagas, the Cayugas, and the Senecas.

Members of all the Iroquois nations sought safety where they could. Some joined Iroquois communities that had long been established in Canada. Two Catholic missions had been founded there in the 17th century by French missionaries who had worked among the Mohawks and other Iroquois. These villages were composed mainly of Mohawks. The settlements, called Kahnawake (gah-na-WA-ge) and Kanesatake (ga-ne-sa-DA-ke), were located near Montreal. Kahnawake, meaning "at the rapids," was situated just south of the city along the southern shore of the St. Lawrence River. Kanesatake, meaning "place of reeds," was located a short distance to the west. A third Catholic Mohawk mission dating from the mid-18th century also drew additional residents after the revolutionary war. This community, called Akwesasne (ah-gwe-ZAS-ne), meaning "where the partridge drums," is situated along the southern shore of the St. Lawrence River approximately 80 miles southwest of Montreal.

In addition to these older communities, some Mohawks set up a new village on land they obtained near the Bay of Quinte, north of Lake Ontario in eastern Ontario. Others joined a contingent of Onondagas, Cayugas, and Senecas who had settled on land, purchased for them by Canadian officials, along the Grand River near Brantford, Ontario. The settlement is located just north of the U.S. border. This large community is called Six Nations because people from all the nations of the confederacy reside there.

After the American Revolution, most Oneidas remained for a time in their villages in New York. Later, in 1838, some Oneidas purchased land in Wisconsin from an Indian group called the Menominees. Oneida land there is located near the city of Green Bay. Other Oneidas sold their remaining territory in New York in 1840. They moved to a site near London, Ontario, west of the city of Toronto.

In 1788, at the Treaty of Fort Schuyler, the Onondagas ceded all of their original land to the state of New York except for 100 square miles along Onondaga Creek, south of Syracuse. During the next half century, parcels of land were sold until the Onondaga community retained only 6,100 acres of their ancient homeland. After the Revolution, a number of Cayugas remained in their village at Cayuga Lake; others journeyed north and settled among the Iroquois at Six Nations along the Grand River.

The Senecas were able to keep some of their homeland in western New York State. By provisions of the Treaty

George Washington, the first American president, firing a cannon at Yorktown, Virginia, in 1781. Two years earlier, Washington had authorized an invasion of Iroquois territory.

of Big Tree, signed in 1797, four Seneca communities became protected reservations. These are known as Buffalo Creek, Cattaraugus, Allegheny, and Tonawanda. Then, in 1838, a number of chiefs agreed to sell most of their land. After vigorous protest by most Senecas, the lands at Allegheny and Cattaraugus were returned in the Compromise Treaty of 1842. In 1857, the Seneca nation bought back the Tonawanda Reservation. Members of the Tuscarora nation retained some land in western New York and maintain a reservation there near Lewiston in Niagara County.

Despite the dislocation of their peoples, the Iroquois Confederacy has struggled to survive. The council fire, which had been covered with ashes in 1777, was rekindled in the next decade at two locations. Confederacy chiefs lit the fire in the Onondaga village at Six Nations in Canada and at the Buffalo Creek Reservation in New York. Two councils were thus established, one in Canada and one in the United States. Each council had its own set of titles. Both shared the treasured wampum belts that had previously been held at Onondaga. When the reservation at Buffalo Creek was sold by the Senecas in 1842, the council fire and wampum belts were transferred to the Onondaga Reservation in central New York State.

On all of the Iroquois reservations (called reserves in Canada), some form of hereditary leadership associated with the confederacy still exists today. However, the role of chiefs in their communities varies. In most places, traditional councils have been replaced as governing bodies by an elected council. In some cases, the majority of the local community approved this change. In other reservations, the state, provincial, or federal government unilaterally imposed an elective system of government.

Confederacy chiefs in council, around 1910. In center, with wampum strings, is Onondaga chief David John.

The Senecas at Allegheny and Cattaraugus enacted a constitution in 1848, which shifted to an elective system of local government. They took this action because of their outrage that hereditary chiefs had agreed to sell the land 10 years before. When the land was returned, the Senecas' distrust of their chiefs continued. However, confederacy chiefs at the other Seneca reservation, Tonawanda, had not agreed to the sale. In fact, they were instrumental in buying back Seneca land. Therefore, Senecas at Tonawanda joined together to keep the traditional system. Their present council is composed of eight league chiefs, eight subchiefs, and three tribal officers who are elected.

At Six Nations, controversies over forms of leadership grew in the late 19th century. A number of prominent Mohawks organized opposition to traditional chiefs. They formed a group called the Dehorners. They took this name after the confederacy ceremony of deposing, or dehorning, league chiefs. Although the Dehorners were vocal in their desire to institute an elective system, many others at Six Nations wanted to keep the traditional council. The community was divided in factions favoring or opposing adoption of Canadian and American practices. Those in favor of changing their basic economic activities tended to advocate an elective system. Those who wanted to maintain more of the traditional lifeways tended to prefer the hereditary leadership. After many years of controversy, the Canadian government unilaterally suspended the confederacy council as the governing body in September 1924. Elections were held the following month.

In 1959, the confederacy chiefs at Six Nations and 1,300 of their supporters marched on the Council Hall and ousted the elected leaders. The RCMP (Royal Canadian Mounted Police) evicted them after one week of occupation, but the issue of leadership at Six Nations still remains controversial.

Only among the Onondagas does the confederacy council continue to function as the sole form of local government. The council there consists of 27 chiefs, including the 14 titled Onondaga league chiefs and 13 assistants. The chief who carries the name of Thadodaho has no assistant.

Among most of the other Iroquois nations, two councils coexist. One consists of elected members who are recognized by state, provincial, and federal authorities. The other consists of hereditary chiefs who are selected according to age-old custom by senior women of the clans. The chiefs are installed and condoled in ceremonies conceived by Hiawatha and the Peacemaker.

The rituals of installation and condolence repeat the speeches and songs of ancient times. They also make note of the passage of time since the days of the founders. In modern condolence councils, a speaker proclaims:

> Oh, my grandsires! Even now that has become old which you established, the Great League. You have it as a pillow under your heads in the ground where you are lying, this Great League which you established; although you said that far away in the future the Great League would endure.

Such speeches indicate the Iroquois' recognition that times and institutions change over the centuries. They also reflect people's attitudes about their own situation and capabilities. In comparison with the days of the founders, conditions for the Iroquois have deteriorated. The position of the confederacy as a flourishing, dominating force in regional and national politics has declined. However, continuity of confederacy rituals ensures the perpetuation of the ideals and aspirations of the founders.

The confederacy continues to be a viable institution, both as a symbol of Iroquois culture and as a focus of

An Iroquois protest in Buffalo, New York, in 1940. The protesters, who were born in Canada, were angered that the U.S. government was compelling them to register as aliens.

political activity today. League chiefs play prominent roles in local and national politics. One issue of great concern to the Iroquois people involves the disposition of the wampum belts that were originally kept at Onondaga. After the American Revolution, Iroquois leaders divided these belts between the council at Six Nations and the one at Buffalo Creek in New York. In 1848, belts held at Buffalo Creek were transferred to the Onondaga Reservation in New York. During the following decades, many of these belts were sold or given away. By 1878, only 12 remained. Four of these were sold in 1891.

Fearing the loss of more wampum, confederacy chiefs gave the belts to the New York State Museum for

safekeeping in 1898. However, by the 1960s, many Iroquois wanted the belts returned to their people. They considered the belts to be symbols of their culture and sovereignty. After much controversy, the New York State legislature enacted a law in 1970 to return the wampum to Onondaga after construction of a facility that would ensure their security. Finally, in a ceremonial transfer, the belts were returned to Onondaga on October 21, 1989. Confederacy chief Thadodaho, a title then held by Leon Shenandoah, accepted the belts in the name of the Iroquois nations.

Three additional wampum belts purchased in 1930 by the Canadian Museum of Civilization were returned to the confederacy in February 1991. In accordance with the responsibility given by Hiawatha and the Peacemaker, Thadodaho once again has the honor of keeping the treasured wampum.

In 1970, the League Council of the Iroquois Nations took a symbolic act by issuing confederacy passports to several Iroquois people who had been invited to attend an international conference in Sweden. Swedish and European authorities acknowledged these passports and

In 1970, a group of Iroquois picket in Albany, New York, demanding the return of nearly 30 wampum belts held by the state.

allowed the Iroquois travelers to use them. However, officials in Great Britain did not permit the people to leave the airport in London. The confederacy council's action made a statement about sovereignty, which is the right of people to govern themselves and determine their way of life.

Confederacy leaders and their supporters have often appeared at the United Nations to appeal for the recognition of rights of Indian peoples in the United States and Canada. They have also joined with many groups in support of land claims and legal and social rights of indigenous peoples in countries throughout the world.

In 1987, the United States Congress officially recognized the influence of the Iroquois and their confederacy on the development of the United States. In preparation for the bicentennial year of the U.S. Constitution, a congressional resolution proclaimed:

The Congress acknowledges the historical debt which this Republic of the United States of America owes to the Iroquois Confederacy for their demonstration of enlightenment, democratic principles of government, and their example of the free association of independent nations.

The importance of the league to its members continues today. The lasting legacy of Hiawatha and the Peacemaker has not been eclipsed with the passage of time or with changes in external circumstances. The confederacy arose at a time of turmoil in order to bring peace to nations in conflict. Its strength derives, in part, from the ability of its people to continue to adapt to changes in their life. The words and ideas of Hiawatha and the Peacemaker are kept alive by the Iroquois, who are their historical and spiritual descendants. The founders said: "Our strength shall be in union. Our way the way of reason, righteousness, and peace."

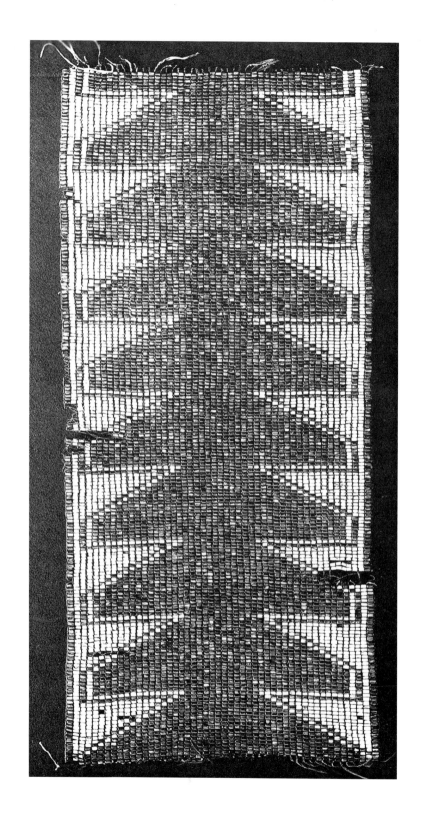

CHRONOLOGY

ca. 1350–1400	Birth of Hiawatha in the village of Onondaga in present-day New York State
ca. 1400–50	Conflict in Onondaga village between Hiawatha and Thadodaho, resulting in Hiawatha's decision to leave Onondaga
ca. 1450	Meeting between Hiawatha and the Peacemaker near a Mohawk village
ca. 1450	Formation of the Iroquois Confederacy by the Five Nations—the Mohawks, the Oneidas, the Onondagas, the Cayugas, and the Senecas
Late 15th century	Death of Hiawatha
Early 17th century	Contact between Iroquois and Europeans (Dutch, British, French)
1614	Establishment of Fort Orange (later Albany) by the Dutch in Mohawk territory
1722	Tuscaroras join the Iroquois Confederacy as the sixth nation
1777	Confederacy Chiefs "cover up the ashes" of the confederacy council fire because of failure to reach a consensus regarding support for the Americans or the British during the revolutionary war
1787	Rekindling of confederacy fire at Onondaga village on the Six Nations Reserve in Ontario and at the Buffalo Creek Reservation in New York
1987	U.S. congressional resolution proclaims the historical influence of the principles of the Iroquois Confederacy in the formulation of the U.S. Constitution
1989	Return of ceremonial wampum belts from the New York State Museum to the Iroquois Confederacy at Onondaga
1991	Return of ceremonial wampum belts from the Canadian Museum of Civilization to the Iroquois Confederacy at Onondaga

FURTHER READING

Colden, Cadwallader. *The History of the Five Indian Nations.* Ithaca, NY: Cornell University Press, 1958.

Cornplanter, Jesse. *Legends of the Longhouse.* Port Washington, NY: Ira Friedman, 1963.

Hale, Horatio. *The Iroquois Book of Rites.* New York: AMS Press, 1969.

Henry, Thomas. *Wilderness Messiah: The Story of Hiawatha and the Iroquois.* New York: William Sloane Associates, 1955.

Hertzberg, Hazel. *The Great Tree and the Longhouse: The Culture of the Iroquois.* New York: Macmillan, 1966.

Johansen, Bruce. *Forgotten Founders.* Ipswich, MA: Gambit, 1982.

Morgan, Lewis. *League of the Iroquois.* New York: Corinth Press, 1962.

Parker, Arthur C. *Parker on the Iroquois.* Syracuse: Syracuse University Press, 1968.

Thompson, Stith. *Tales of North American Indians.* Bloomington: Indiana University Press, 1960.

Wallace, Paul. *The White Roots of Peace.* Philadelphia: University of Pennsylvania Press, 1946.

INDEX

ACKNOWLEDGMENTS

I wish to thank Mr. Ernest Benedict of Akwesasne for his generous help in reading and commenting on a draft of this book. And I would like to dedicate the book to the descendants of Hiawatha and followers of his message of unity and peace.
—Dr. Nancy Bonvillain

PICTURE CREDITS

NANCY BONVILLAIN is an adjunct professor at the Graduate Faculty, New School for Social Research. She has a Ph.D. in anthropology from Columbia University. Dr. Bonvillain has written a grammar and dictionary of the Mohawk language as well as *The Huron* (1989) and *The Mohawk* (1992) for Chelsea House Publishers. She has also edited *Studies in Iroquois Culture* (1980). Dr. Bonvillain has received grants from the National Endowment for the Humanities, the National Museum of Canada, and the American Philosophical Society for her research in 17th- and 18th-century Iroquoian history.

W. DAVID BAIRD is the Howard A. White Professor of History at Pepperdine University in Malibu, California. He holds a Ph.D. from the University of Oklahoma and was formerly on the faculty of history at the University of Arkansas, Fayetteville, and Oklahoma State University. He has served as president of both the Western History Association, a professional organization, and Phi Alpha Theta, the international honor society for students of history. Dr. Baird is also the author of *The Quapaw Indians: A History of the Downstream People* and *Peter Pitchlynn: Chief of the Choctaws* and the editor of *A Creek Warrior of the Confederacy: The Autobiography of Chief G. W. Grayson.*